THE **OTHER**
EMMELINE

THE **OTHER** EMMELINE

THE STORY OF EMMELINE PETHICK-LAWRENCE

JANE GRANT

Francis
Boutle
Publishers

First published in 2023 by
Francis Boutle Publishers
272 Alexandra Park Road
London N22 7BG
Tel/Fax: (020) 8889 8087
Email: info@francisboutle.co.uk
www.francisboutle.co.uk

The Other Emmeline © Jane W. Grant 2023

ISBN 978 1 7398955 6 3

Contents

Emmeline Pethick-Lawrence 1867-1954

Acknowledgements

I have reason to be grateful to a number of people for their help in writing this book, above all Kathy Atherton, not only for her own books, but for generously sharing her expertise and contacts in the Surrey Hills, and alongside her Ann Nash for sharing her enthusiasm for the Mascot, where she lives. I am grateful to the Committee of Peaslake Village Hall for making it easy for me to take photos of the painting of Emmeline and Fred by John Baker which has lived in the Hall since 1962; and the staff of the Dorking Museum and Heritage Centre for their help.

Gillian Murphy of the Women's Library at the LSE has been consistently generous and helpful, not only over the manuscript but over the launch of the book; and thanks also to all her colleagues in the Women's Library for so generously sponsoring the book launch. I am also very grateful to Anne Summers and the Friends of The Women's Library; Sandy Paul and Adam Green from the Wren Library at Trinity College Cambridge; Suzanne Keyte of the Royal Albert Hall; and Mari Takayangi of the Parliamentary Archives. My thanks also to the Wellcome Institute, and Beverley Cook, Lluis Tembleque and Nikki Braunton of the Museum Of London

Thank you also to Wendi Momen, Brian Harrison, Ali Ronan, Helen Kay Charlotte Bill , Judge Smith and Jan Pethick and all the members of the Women's International League of Peace and Freedom (WILPF) who went to Zurich in April 2019 to recreate the Peace Congress a hundred years earlier.

And finally a big thank you for all the family support: to Tara for being my 'eyes' in Zurich and looking after me over my many visits to the Wren Library in Cambridge, to Alex for fierce but necessary editing and to Neville for rescuing the footnotes and chasing up the pictures – a time-consuming and heroic venture.

And thanks to my publisher Clive Boutle for all his support.

Weston-super-Mare in the 1890s, sometimes simply called "Weston".
The young Emmeline Pethick described her home town as "a limited little
world." She had a strong urge to reach out to a wider world.

List of Illustrations

All illustrations are from the Women's Library at the LSE unless otherwise stated in caption box

Preface

Even given the relative popularity of the name Emmeline in the late Victorian period, it is still a curious coincidence that two leaders of the the movement for women's suffrage at the beginning of the twentieth century should share the same first name. Emmeline Pankhurst, of course, needs no introduction. She was, with her daughter Christabel, the founder and poster girl of the Women's Social and Political Union (WSPU). Until the First World War she was everywhere, and was quoted everywhere. And she died in the thick of the suffrage struggle in 1928, before the passing of the Equal Franchise Act, which at last gave women the same voting rights as men. So her reputation has had little chance to fade, and it was bolstered by a striking statue erected in Victoria Tower Gardens in 1930.

The life and reputation of Emmeline Pethick-Lawrence were more nuanced. Her background was similar to Pankhurst's in many ways. Born on 21 October 1867 into a middle-class family, Emmeline Pethick worked as a social worker, and she had left-wing leanings, a very happy marriage, and an immense commitment to women's suffrage. Emmeline Pethick-Lawrence's commitment and contribution may have been less flamboyant than Emmeline Pankhurst's, but it was none the less essential. Given the poor state of the WSPU in 1906, it is highly likely that without Emmeline Pethick-Lawrence's phenomenal fund-raising and organisational skills the Union would not have become a viable organisation, let alone such a successful one. And she also contributed creativity, oratory, courage – she was imprisoned several times – and leadership. She and her husband shared their houses, their gardens and their money with the movement, with great generosity. It was Emmeline Pethick-Lawrence – not Millicent Fawcett or the Pankhursts – who first conceived the suffrage movement's iconic Purple, White and Green colours, which have characterised the movement ever since.

In 1901 Emmeline married Frederick Lawrence, who later served as a Labour MP, and briefly Leader of the Opposition during the Second World War. Subsequently, he was Secretary of State for India and Burma 1945-1947, where he tried valiantly to secure a peaceful transition to independence. Theirs was a partnership of equals. Once the

Pethick-Lawrences were ejected from the WSPU in 1912, for reasons that are complex and still contested (see Chapter 4), they continued to edit *Votes for Women*, while Emmeline went on to campaign for peace with the same passion as she had shown in campaigning for the vote. She was a major player in the women's peace movement from 1915 onwards, participating in the peace conferences in The Hague in 1915 and in Zurich in 1919. These two conferences were important landmarks of women's involvement in the First World War and should be given more prominence in the many histories of the war written in the century since. They have also had an interesting afterlife in the women's and peace movements of the twenty-first century.

In the last few years the Women's International League of Peace and Freedom (WILPF) has organised two centennial conferences – one in 2015, entitled 'Women's Power to Stop War: Uniting a Global Movement', to celebrate their initial founding at the conference in the Hague in 1915, and one in Zurich in 2019 to celebrate the International Congress of Women held in that city in 1919, at which WILPF was fully established.

The afterlife of these two commemorative conferences has been extended through the making of two short films by Charlotte Bill which have been widely shown to great acclaim. The first, *These Dangerous Women*, concentrated on the abortive journey of the British women to The Hague, played by present-day members of WILPF, including their wait on the docks at Tilbury for ships that never arrived. As it was wartime the British government had closed the Channel and North Sea to all civilian shipping, so only three British women, one of whom was Emmeline, made it to the Hague in 1915.

I was one of a sizable contingent of WILPF members from the UK who attended the 2015 conference at the Peace Palace at The Hague alongside many WILPF members from across Europe. Another tranche of funding led to both a second commemorative conference and a second film (Versailles 1919: Return of the Dangerous Women). This funding meant that large contingents from each country could attend a follow-up conference at Zurich in 2019 dressed as the original 1919 participants (I attended it myself in the character of Emmeline Pethick-Lawrence, wearing a big black hat).

The Zurich conference of 2019 wasn't just a fancy-dress party: it demonstrated a strong commitment to the cause of peace, and an empathetic connection with the dedicated women who struggled for a genuine, lasting peace to emerge from the First World War.

This conference took place in the very same hotel, the Glockenhof, where the women had met in 1919, with delegates from the US and

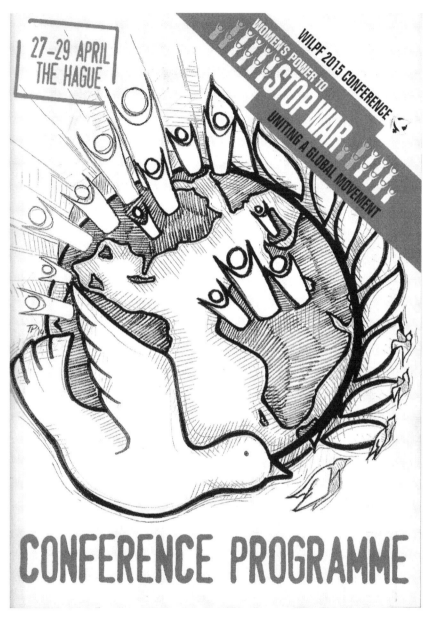

Conference programme. The original conference in 1915 was to try to stop World War 1. The re-enactment in 2015 was to try to unite a global movement to stop all war.

many European countries. There were wonderful scenes in the film including the British women braving the wind to display their PEACE banner on a ferry from Dover to Calais. There was a special moment when the delegate from France arrived late at Zurich to be greeted with flowers and an embrace from the delegate from Germany. This was European peace and harmony at its best. It was almost too poignant as the conference took place under the shadow of the Brexit negotiations and as UK was leaving the European Union.

Emmeline Pethick-Lawrence would have been pleased and proud that her message for peace had been so cogently articulated a hundred years after the conferences in which she played so prominent a part.

Unfortunately this message has been articulated very little in books about the First World War – nothing in Liddell Hart, almost nothing in Max Hastings – only Adam Hochschild and Margaret Macmillan gave women peace campaigners the prominence they deserve.

So in a rather inappropriate phrase 'la lutta continua': the campaign to achieve peace can and must continue. These conferences are important because they show hope is possible and that peace can be envisioned even if the effect on world events at the time might be close to zero. This is a powerful legacy from Emmeline.

She then played a heroic role in publicising the brutal activities of the Black and Tans during the Irish War of Independence. She subsequently held leadership roles in a number of equality organisations, such as Charlotte Despard's Women's Freedom League and Lady Rhondda's Six Point Group. But her public involvement grew less as her health and her hearing deteriorated, and by the 1930s she had largely withdrawn to live in her house in Surrey, where she died in 1954.

Ironically, the fact she lived so much longer than Emmeline Pankhurst probably was a factor in her fall into relative obscurity. While Pankhurst was widowed early, with four young children, Emmeline Pethick-Lawrence's happy marriage to a successful man who outlived her may also have contributed, as it made her later history less dramatic. Her autobiography, *My Part in a Changing World*, published by Victor Gollancz in 1938, is long out of print, and following her death little was written about her until very recently. This book is intended to bring her back to centre stage, where she deserves to be.

Note

To avoid confusion I frequently refer to Emmeline Pankhurst as Mrs Pankhurst, the name by which she was widely known, whereas any reference to 'Emmeline' alone refers to Emmeline Pethick-Lawrence unless it is associated with the Pankhurst daughters, Sylvia and Christabel. Frederick Pethick-Lawrence is called Fred, which was the name he was most frequently known by, throughout.

Abbreviations

WSPU – Women's Social and Political Union
WILPF – Women's International League of Peace and Freedom

1. Early Years

On 21 October 1867 Emmeline Pethick was born into a large middle-class evangelical family in Clifton, Bristol. Her father Henry was a businessman – a merchant of South African hides – and he was later the owner of the *Western Gazette* newspaper, a Weston-Super-Mare town commissioner, and a county magistrate.

Although Emmeline was comfortably off, even before she met her rich husband Fred Lawrence, her childhood was not particularly happy. She explained in her autobiography, *My Part in a Changing World*, how she experienced the Victorian sphere of the nursery as a prison with nursemaids as gaolers (this was to reverberate with her when she was later imprisoned as a suffragette). She had a much more positive relationship with the family's cook Charlotte, who ruled in the kitchen for many years, and she had an affectionate relationship with her mother, Fanny (née Collen) who was 'a fund of quiet wisdom' and 'a very gracious person'.[1]

But this was blighted by her mother's continuous childbearing and the death of so many of Emmeline's siblings: only eight out of a total of thirteen survived infancy. Those who survived included her sisters Annie, May, Marie and Dorothy, who later became very active with Emmeline in the suffragette movement, and her brothers Frank, Harry and Tom.

Emmeline's father may have been in some respects a typical authoritarian Victorian father, but he had progressive views on religion, and 'a deep strain of religious mysticism'.[2] He was very fond of young people, and he was considered a rebel, with a strong love of justice. Emmeline adored him.

Emmeline's early life was punctuated by trips to church (although she was very much 'puzzled by God'), and attendance at a kindergarten (where she longed to be picked by the biggest boy to march round the room, but was constantly pipped to the post by a girl with golden hair, called Dimple). Holidays were spent at the seaside, either at Weston-Super-Mare, on the Somerset coast, or Penarth, near Cardiff. It was at Penarth that she was once cut off by the tide and had to be rescued by fishermen in a boat.

When Emmeline was eight she was sent to a boarding school in

Devizes, Greystone House, where the punishment of being 'sent to Coventry' seemed to follow every minor misdemeanour, and 'an attitude of suspicion and accusation' prevailed. Her stay at Miss Bidwell's – the school was known after its headmistress – was finally brought to a close when she contracted rheumatic fever and was sent home. Things got better after that. For a start she was sent to day school and the family moved from Clifton to a more child-friendly house in Weston-super-Mare, 20 miles from Bristol. The house had wide lawns, a magnificent kitchen garden, miles of countryside to explore and, best of all, a recalcitrant donkey in a field.

To these delights were later added the new, revolutionary bicycles for girls, tennis courts built in the field, and a hockey team, all organised by her father. At the same time he was organising a petition against the persecution of members of the Salvation Army, whose doctrine of practical Christianity – soup, soap and salvation, with its quasi-military structure and uniforms – was intended to encourage both social and spiritual transformation amongst society's poorest and most marginalised. This attracted considerable hostility, 1882 being their worst year in terms of persecution, with riots and disorders taking place unchecked by the police.[3]

The fact that her father stood up for the Salvation Army earned him 'forever afterwards' Emmeline's 'ardent gratitude and admiration' for standing up against injustice. He was later to display the same response to injustice when Emmeline was arrested and imprisoned as a suffragette.

Emmeline was later sent as a boarder to a local 'Finishing School', where she was, surprisingly, accepted in spite of her family being classified as the dreaded 'trade' – a category beneath contempt amongst the local upper classes. She was subsequently sent, with her sister Annie, to board at a school in Nancy, France, where they had 'the jolliest life possible' but learnt very little French. A trip to a school in Wiesbaden with her sister May (who managed to contract scarlet fever there) resulted, in the end, in as much fun, but she also learnt some German. Returning home to Weston she found it difficult to settle in spite of her constant devotion to her surviving siblings (particularly her youngest brother Frank, with whom she was united in 'permanent friendship and love'), and she began to feel vaguely restless and dissatisfied with her position.

> I had grown up under the influence of prevailing ideas. At first I had taken it for granted that as a woman I should be supported all my life, first by my father and later on by a

husband… But now I began to be weighed down in spirit, by the fact of my dependence.[4]

In the 1880s, even middle-class women had no independence. Admittedly, Emmeline's cage in middle class Weston-super-Mare was a gilded one, but there were few ways out. Even if she were able to get a paid job, she would be taking away the livelihood of a much poorer woman, or indeed a man, as an essential bread winner. The societally more acceptable route was, of course, marriage, but 'There were too many girls in Weston, far too many.'

> Marriage as an abstract proposition held no attraction for me. In fact to marry and settle down in Weston seemed in some ways even less desirable than the present position, because it would close all doors to deliverance from our limited little world.[5]

The alternative was to be trapped at home in the role of unmarried daughter in a dependent position and one of her main instincts at this stage was the need to leave home. Surprisingly, a flirtation with a visiting young naval officer – which went nowhere since he had no money – 'planted new seeds of courage and self-confidence in my heart'.[6]

It addressed her shyness, made her feel attractive for the first time, and gave her confidence that she could find people who could give her friendship and love.

Emmeline was already being exposed to new ideas through her friend Mabelle Pearse, who took her to meetings in London of the Fellowship or the New Life, of which the future prime Minister James Ramsay MacDonald was a member, at the Inns of Court (the fellowship disbanded in 1898 but its offshoot, the Fabian Society, of course very much lives on). Words like 'wage-slaves' and 'wage-slavery' were freely used in these meetings, feeding Emmeline's later commitment to socialism and social justice. These ideas from the Fellowship – of the cultivation of a perfect character in each and all – were not well-received at home.

The need to escape from the 'restricted lives of girls of the leisured middle classes' became more acute, and in 1890 Emmeline left for London, and a new life, at the age of 23. She was able to negotiate a role as a voluntary sister-in-charge of the Working Girls' Club, mainly for girls involved in the clothing trade, led by Katherine Price Hughes of the West London Methodist Mission. Emmeline's role took her across a large chunk of central London: 'our district ran north and south from Marylebone Road to Soho and east to west from Tottenham Court Road to Regent Street.'[7]

The City 'Mission' movement was at its height at the end of the nineteenth century. The West London Methodist Mission had been set up in 1887 by Hugh Price Hughes, husband of Katherine, to offer both spiritual and practical support for poor people in West London (its mission today remains very similar – 'to empower people affected by homelessness, poverty and trauma').

Emmeline's introduction to her new life was a shock, and she found conditions at the mission to be harsh. But the reaction of disapproval from her community back home was worse:

> The very idea that women should leave their homes and live in the comparative freedom of a community, in order to carry out rather subversive principles of social sharing, was a bombshell to the large mass of conservative low-church and non-conformist opinion.[8]

This hostility spurred her on to make a success of her new job. The woman who was to become her greatest friend, the strong-minded and idiosyncratic Mary Neal, from Bournemouth, had been sent home sick, leaving the challenging Working Girls' Club at Cleveland Hall, Cleveland Street, in a very disorganised state. Emmeline was thrown in at the deep end and sent to take it over. Using the experience gained from entertaining her younger brothers and sisters at home, she managed to build up some rapport with young girls working for very low wages in the clothing trade. When Mary returned to the club, she found that she and Emmeline had the same ideas about their shared work:

> We thought of it not only as an attempt to help individuals to a happier and more successful life, but also as a field for study and an opportunity of working out new ideas which, if they proved successful, would pave the way for greater things.[9]

Their ideas were to strongly influence the development of the university settlement movement and they, in turn, were influenced by the 'gospel of socialism' as preached by Keir Hardie, the leader of the Independent Labour Party, and the philosopher and mystical poet Edward Carpenter (an English Utopian Socialist, a pacifist and an early campaigner for gay rights).

The Mission was one of the few places where young, mostly middle-class women could acquire both a 'degree of autonomy and a sense of effecting change in a wider sphere'.[10]

Working unpaid as 'Sister Emmeline', one of their 'Sisters of the People', was (as for her friend Mary Neal) an eye-opener for Emmeline.[11] Katherine Price Hughes saw the Sisterhood as having a double purpose, as both supporting the poor and giving opportunities for educated young women:

> The idea of the Sisterhood had long been in my mind as I wondered if it were possible to form some organisation which would reach the educated women of our own Church, I thought especially of those who were not obliged to earn their own living and who remained at home after leaving school with practically nothing to do and simply longing to have some outlet for their energies and a purpose in life. Very few were the doors open to women and the chains of early Victorian repression still bound them and still more firmly bound them to their parents.[12]

Coming from a sheltered middle-class family, Emmeline had absolutely no idea about the destitution of the urban poor, who were forced to work for long hours at starvation wages, and to live in appallingly over-crowded housing, with only the workhouse as any sort of safety net. Emmeline became particularly obsessed by the need for a scheme of national insurance and a Widowed Mothers' Pension, and she spent much time fighting for these throughout her life, with some success. Though she was appalled by the conditions in which the girls from the Club were forced to live, she was constantly impressed by 'the high spirits of the young and the recklessness of the oppressed', and was determined that they should not become so down-trodden and brow-beaten as their mothers, who were often ground down by poverty and violent marriages.

Opportunities for entertainment were very few, apart from the pub. Emmeline and Mary tried their best to insert some fun into their club evenings, but they soon realized that what the girls needed was a long week's holiday in the country. This had never been done before, and it proved very difficult to organise and raise money for – at a time when holidays away for the working poor, apart from day-trips to the seaside, were almost unheard of. But in the end a group of girls were transported to the countryside for a week's stay. Later on the Green Lady

Hostel was established at Littlehampton, with the charitable help of the Jewish philanthropists Lilian and Marion Montagu, who were trying to do the same for the girls in the large Jewish Club they ran, and the result was transformational:

> Every day was a new experience. They had never known quietness. They had never seen the stars. They had never plucked a flower. They had never heard the cuckoo, and when they heard it for the first time they began looking for the clock.[13]

In her autobiography, Emmeline mused on the changes that have taken place for the better, once her husband Fred, who served as Financial Secretary to the Treasury in a Labour government in 1929, had been instrumental in ensuring that at least all manual workers in government service got a full week's holiday with pay. She concludes:

> I like to dwell upon the scope of these changes because I am strengthened in my belief that there is no vision or dream too good to come true, The dream must be definitely conceived and brought into the physical world by a courageous effort, however small the actual achievement may be. When once incarnated the idea will make its own way and, sooner or later, will find universal acceptance.[14]

Emmeline seems to have been extremely happy at this stage of her life. In October 1891 she gave her first public speech at the anniversary celebrations of the West London Mission and she realised that she had a 'new power, the exercise of which has been a great joy through the whole course of my life',[15] and one which was certainly to be exercised extensively.

There were new friendships, particularly with Kathleen Fitzpatrick, an intense Irish girl who ran an inspirational mission for children. Emmeline describes a trip to St Ives in Cornwall with three friends and a walking tour in the Alps with another new friend, Marie, in almost ecstatic terms – an intimation of the seam of mysticism she experienced throughout her life. Emmeline was certainly extremely optimistic, and buoyant, at this point in her life:

> It was a wonderful thing at that period to be young among young comrades, for the ninth decade of the last century was a time of expansion and vision…Trade Unionism was

winning its early victories, food was becoming more plen-
tiful and cheaper, and we did not question the reality of
progress as we do to-day. It was the day, also, of prophets
and poets who foretold a new heaven and a new earth and
indicated the steps by which they could be obtained. It
was an era of religion and faith, and at the same tine of
intellectual challenge. We read, discussed, debated and
experimented and felt that all life lay before us to be
changed and moulded by our vision and desire.[16]

On a less exalted level, Emmeline and Mary Neal were becoming
disenchanted with the 'unnatural institutional life', the environment of
Katherine House (part of the West London Mission) where 'as time
went on the house in which we lived settled down into a quite comfortable middle-class household with servants and regular solid meals'.
These and other restrictions of the West London Mission (including its
puritanical aversion to dancing and drama) made it less appealing, and
the Mission, in turn, was becoming disenchanted with them.
Accordingly, in August 1895 Emmeline and Mary left it and went independent, in order to establish a 'social service of a new pattern' on the
basis that 'only by living amongst the people and being one of them
could one establish real, as apart from professional, friendship'.

The most disturbing part of this move was that it initially caused a
break with the preacher Mark Guy Pearse – originally a friend of
Emmeline's father – who had been Emmeline's mentor since she was
a child and who had co-founded the West London Mission with his
friend Price Hughes.

Emmeline had known Pearse since she was twelve. Pearse was born
in 1842, which made him 25 years older than Emmeline. He was a
charismatic Cornishman who had come to London in 1861 to study
medicine at St. Bartholomew's Hospital. He subsequently gave up
being a medical student to become a renowned Methodist preacher
and lecturer, and a prolific author of devotional works and semi-reli-
gious tales.[17]

He was married and had a large number of children of around
Emmeline's own age.

Fortunately, this breach was healed and Pearse went on to become a
firm supporter of Emmeline and Mary, who were struggling to live in a
tiny flat off the Euston Road on a combined income of £80 a year
(which was a small amount even in those days).

Emmeline and Mary were also struggling to establish the independent Esperance Club from their flat, with its emphasis on young work-

ing girls and women, and on activities such as holidays in the country. The Club also included a co-operative dressmaking establishment called the Maison Esperance, which provided seamstresses – a notoriously underpaid and exploited part of the workforce – with decently paid, year-round employment. The new venture was much supported by the donations of John Passmore Edwards (another Cornishman and former Liberal MP, publisher, lifelong champion of the working classes, and benefactor, particularly of hospitals and libraries).

Emmeline remained involved with the Maison Esperance even after her marriage to Fred Lawrence in 1901, but less so with the folk songs and Morris dancing which Mary Neal subsequently developed for the girls with Herbert McIlwaine (who became the Club's musical director), the folk-song collector Cecil Sharp, and the Morris dancer William Kimber. At one level this was a huge success: the girls took very enthusiastically to both the songs and dancing, performed regularly in public, and some of them even started teaching Morris dancing to others. But there was, from the start, an element of jealousy between Mary and the men involved. Mary saw Morris dancing as a 'channel down which life-giving creative power would flow', but she perceived Cecil Sharp's vision 'as creating by dance and gesture, a vortex of power which if misused could become evil and destructive'. This level of misogyny is found in many similar organisations both then and since. Mary saw the dispute as a battle between the sexes: 'I had broken the law of a cosmic ritual. I had put women into a masculine rhythm when I taught girls to dance the Morris and Sword dances.'[18]

But Mary Neal was to spend the rest of her life fighting for Morris dancing, with little personal recognition. Her contribution to the folk music and dance movement was overshadowed by Sharp, who became the central figure of the narrative, and the revered authority.[19]

If Mary Neal was breaking away into dance, Emmeline was breaking away in two directions – into marriage, and into the suffragette movement. Both these two developments would turn out to be mutually reinforcing rather than in conflict. In spite of their different pathways, Emmeline and Mary remained great friends all their lives. Emmeline's years as an inspirational youth worker, alongside Mary, were to influence the rest of her life. Mary later introduced Emmeline to an idealistic youth organisation, the Fellowship of the Kibbo Kift, and Mary went down to Surrey to spend her last few years living close to Emmeline until her death in 1944.

2. Fred

For someone who had been very ambivalent about marriage, in the event Emmeline embraced the institution with enthusiasm. There seemed to be a sort of inevitability about her union with Frederick Lawrence (who was always known simply as Fred). They first met in 1899, when they worked backstage at a play put on by the Settlement movement, in which Fred also worked. On her way home on the train afterwards with Mary Neal, Mary stated 'Emmeline, I feel sure that you are going to marry that man'. Emmeline was taken aback:

> I was rather shocked at this remark, because in our position amongst our fellow workers we had always considered it necessary to avoid any such talk, and I had never known her to break this unwritten rule.[1]

Fred's background was in some respects very similar to Emmeline's, although he was four years younger than her, and richer. He was born in 1871 into a large, prosperous, Unitarian family, living in Paddington. His grandfather William Lawrence had been a self-made 'Dick Whittington' who had come to London from Cornwall as a carpenter at the age of nineteen in 1809. He went on to become a master-builder and the head of the firm William Lawrence & Sons, as well as Sheriff of the City of London – his fortunes were much enhanced by the extension of Cannon Street in 1853. The associated firm Lawrence Brothers Smiths and Founders, part of the City Iron Works, was subsequently run by two more brothers, Alfred and Frederick. Fred's father Alfred died as a result of a freak accident – bumping into a column at a railway station and sustaining head injuries – when Fred was very young, but Fred grew up surrounded by a loving mother and many kind aunts and uncles (his father was one of eleven children, and Fred himself had four siblings).

But inevitably, given his gender, Fred had a very different experience of education from Emmeline's rather spasmodic attendance at school. At eleven he was sent as a boarder to Wixenford preparatory school in Berkshire, and thereafter he went to Eton and Trinity College, Cambridge. He did well at all three: as he explained in his autobiography,[2] 'I do not remember a time when I was not fond of figures.'[3]

But he was not spectacular at mathematics at Wixenford, and when he got to Eton he found its arcane traditions confusing and often elitist. He found the teaching of classics deplorable, but he was at last able to shine at mathematics:

> When it came to mathematics I was one of the exceptions who understood what it was all about, and occasionally in my later years, when I was in a privileged position, I used to put conundrums to the masters... Each year the boys with a mathematical bent competed for the Tomline Prize. I was the third in the line.[4]

Fred also took to science with great enthusiasm and, as time went by, he worked his way up the various Eton hierarchies and eventually became Captain of Oppidans (as the non-scholars were called), with various privileges, such as addressing an aged Queen Victoria when she came on a visit to Eton, and being presented to an equally aged (and very deaf) William Gladstone when he came to give a talk on Homer.

After he left Eton, Fred concluded that he had been very unhappy at times. But however hard it was to defend the privilege, he had clearly benefited from his time there.

> There is no doubt that from the standpoint of worldly promotion my Eton schooldays have been of incalculable benefit to me in after life. Etonians have stood by me when I was vigorously attacking their privileges and their preconceived ideas. Also the experience that I gained at Eton has given me an approach to men and affairs which has been invaluable to me both in business and politics.[5]

Fred went straight from Eton to Trinity College, Cambridge, as a scholar. He spent six years of 'unclouded satisfaction' studying Mathematical Tripos. One reason for his satisfaction was the prominence that Trinity gave to mathematics, 'the premier subject at Cambridge'. He thrived on the problems set by his tutor, and he confidently affirmed that

> The real fact is that mathematics is the medium through which our imagination works. It is the form which our mental images take and the expression of our intellectual activity. On the one hand it presents the world to us

objectively; in hard outline; on the other, it is itself to us adventure, poetry, romance and in a sense mystic religion.[6]

In 1894 Fred was presented for the examination of Mathematical Tripos and gained First Class Honours, as 'fourth wrangler'. He then decided to stay on and take Part I of the Natural Sciences Tripos (in physics, chemistry, mineralogy and geology), and on the strength of his physics and chemistry, he emerged with a double first in Mathematics and Natural Sciences. In his fifth year he added economics, under Alfred Marshall, to his list of subjects, winning the Adam Smith prize for an essay 'on an investigation into local variations in wages,' based on research visits round the country.

At the same time Fred was climbing his way up the hierarchies of university politics, as he had done at Eton, ending up as president of the Cambridge Union Society. It was in this capacity that he attended a debate at the Oxford Union on a proposal to allow women to become full members of the University and obtain degrees, 'which after some hesitation I had decided to support'. He also engaged enthusiastically in various sports: billiards, running, football, lawn tennis, and even skating on the frozen river Cam. And he explored various religious organisations and ministries, from the Non-conformist Union to the Congregationalist ministry and the Unitarian foundation's Manchester College in Oxford.

In 1895 Fred travelled with his sister Annie (1863-1953) to the USA, where he met the renowned feminist Jane Addams.[7] As the time to leave Trinity approached he applied to become a fellow, and he was eventually awarded a fellowship, thus ensuring a lifetime's relationship with his old college – and the placing of his archives in Trinity's Wren Library after his death.

On leaving Cambridge Fred decided not to become a don but to use his experience there as the 'gateway to a larger life'. With money from the family's building business he embarked, like many rich young men before him, on a round-the-world trip, starting in India. There he stayed with a variety of friends, mainly from Trinity, who were posted all over the sub-Continent, and he began what was to be a lifelong and passionate interest in the country. He worked on the calculations for the total eclipse of the sun which crossed India in January 1898, and he went on to Ceylon, Australia, New Zealand, and Hong Kong. From Hong Kong he went on to Canton and Shanghai in China, finding in Chinese art 'the life spirit which lies beyond the external form'.[8]

He then went to Japan, where he found both its pretty pre-industrial towns, and its mountain ranges, including the iconic Fujiyama, enchanting. He returned via Honolulu and the Pacific coast of the USA, visiting Yosemite and Yellowstone Park, where he felt almost drunk on geysers, as the following little verse reveals:

Geysers lofty, geysers low,
Geysers rapid, geysers slow;

Geysers gentle, geysers rough,
We thank the Lord we've had enough.

By now he had been joined by his sister Annie and he took her to San Francisco, before crossing America by train, admiring the Niagara Falls in the snow and visiting friends in Washington and the eastern States. They finally embarked on an Atlantic liner bound for England on 1 January 1899. Now was the time for Fred to face up to real life. 'My wander year was over and with it ended my long period of preparation for life. To what purpose should I devote it?' he asked.[9]

On his return to England Fred was struck by the appalling gulf between rich and poor, and by the efforts of a dedicated few to try and do something about it. By a rather different route to Emmeline's, he came to the Settlement movement via the work of the Economics Professor Alfred Marshall (from Trinity College) and Percy Alden (the warden of the Mansfield House University Settlement in Canning Town). He found it hard to reconcile the economics he had learnt in Cambridge with the stark realities of poverty on the ground, but he accepted an invitation to live in the settlement at Canning Town, east London. He totally immersed himself in its life, became its treasurer, and made a point of sampling sleeping conditions in the common dormitory of the settlement's Wave Lodging House. He ran the men's club and gave them a billiard table, on which he played an exhibition match with the winner of the annual tournament.

As Fred was simultaneously reading for the Bar he sometimes acted as a 'poor man's lawyer', gave 'At Homes' at the settlement residence for people living nearby, and took groups of visitors to popular art exhibitions at West Ham Public Hall. He met a variety of labour leaders, usually considered by popular opinion to be agitators, including the 'gentle, quiet' Keir Hardie. The 1890s saw the formation of the Labour Party, and although Fred was persuaded by his uncle Edwin to stand for parliament in North Lambeth as a Liberal Unionist. In the event he did not stand.

It was in the midst of all this activity that Fred first met 'Sister

Emmie' at a theatrical production (describing it as 'love at first sight') in 1899 at which he lent his coat to replace a missing 'property'. He followed up their first encounter with a further meeting in her flat:

> Emmeline Pethick, as all the world was to come to know later, was a woman of deep spiritual feeling. She had dedicated herself to social service; and while she had no prejudice against marriage she saw with unerring judgement that neither she nor her mate could ever really be happy if the yoke by which they were united chafed in such a way as to prevent fulfilment of the complete personality of either.[10]

Attempts to find whether they had that 'fundamental outlook of unity'[11] meant that his courtship was interrupted by struggles with bouts of sleeplessness and depression as he struggled to decide what was the right thing to do. In 1899 Fred eventually managed to satisfy his obsession with ethical issues raised by the South African War (known as the Boer War), where two white civilisations competed (at the expense of the black communities…). In this, he was partly spurred on by his developing relationship with Emmeline. In 1901 he

Barberton Camp in the hot low veld area of the Transvaal in an area now named Mpumalanga. This was one of the over 40 concentration camps set up by the British in the South African War (1899–1902) to hold Boer families to prevent them from assisting the Boer combatants.

Johannesburg Camp: The camps held tens of thousand of old men, women and children, often in terrible conditions. Over 26,000 women and children died in the camps.

visited South Africa, where he met the writer Olive Schreiner (author of *The Story of an African Farm*). He was deeply affected by her feminist (and anti-war) views, and returned home decisively pro-Boer. He also mtet Emily Hobhouse who was deeply moved by the conditions in the concentration camps. She formed an organisation called the South African Wonmen's and Children's Distress Fund, and Fred became the honorary secretary. Emily Hobhouse visted camps in person to distribute the funds raised, which significanltly helped to alleviate hardship. He had also 'felt it incumbent upon me to come to a conclusion in my general attitude to the order and society in which I lived'.[12]

While in South Africa he had read widely (including the works of Mazzini, the Italian revolutionary), thought deeply, and subjected himself to a form of auto-psychoanalysis. His move to the Left was undoubtedly influenced by Emmeline. In a letter to him written in 1900, a year before their marriage, Emmeline wrote passionately of her commitment to socialism:

> Is not an idea in my head – it is in my bones – it was born
> in me – my whole life long it has been my touch-stone –
> my Standard of values. I mean this – my first conscious-
> ness was the clearest, strongest and most inveterate sense
> of the dignity and worth of the human body and soul
> above everything else – and this has forced me into a life-
> long campaign against every sort of bondage, against all
> sorts of established authorities.[13]

This was clearly not compatible with Fred standing for parliament as a Liberal Unionist in North Lambeth, and he finally abandoned his candidacy there. The next time he stood for parliament was in Leicester West in 1923, as a Labour candidate.

After his return from South Africa Fred met Emily Hobhouse (1860-1926), a British Welfare campaigner, anti-war activist and pacifist chiefly remembered for campaigning to improve the appalling conditions for women and children in the concentration camps created for the Boers in the South African War.[14]

Fred also took on some speaking and writing commitments on housing problems. But his most ambitious venture was to take on financial responsibility for the failing Liberal London evening paper, the *Echo*. Founded in the 1860s, the *Echo* had a distinguished past but was no longer going strong. Having little experience in either business or journalism, Fred called on many of his friends to help him in this venture. Amongst those who accepted and came:

> There was one … who brought with her to our delibera-
> tions deep human instinct and practical common sense.
> She brought also two eyes whose glance penetrated to my
> inmost being. Emmeline Pethick and I met once more,
> not only on the committee but at the girls' club of which
> she was President. She took me again to the tiny flat in
> Somerset Terrace, close to St Pancras Church, where I
> had made my original proposal; and the fires of love for
> one another that had lain dormant blazed out afresh and
> illumined our lives, in our hearts on that day in May 1901
> the equal miracle of human love was manifested to us
> with its rich pageantry of light and joy. Henceforward we
> knew that we belonged to one another. We knew that
> whatever gifts we each had were no longer separately our
> own but were part of our common possession. The full
> tide of life had returned. And thus we plighted our troth.[15]

As part of his preparation for marriage Fred paid a visit to his prospective in-laws in Weston-super-Mare. Coming from a smaller immediate family himself, he was overwhelmed by the warm welcome from the Pethick family, including numerous aunts and uncles and 'no less than fifty first cousins'. Fred was particularly struck by the welcome he received from his future father-in law, Henry Pethick, who instructed his daughter, 'I would much rather he treated me as an equal and held his own ground in argument,'[16] marking the start of a lifelong friendship between the two men.

Fred's comparative reticence on his feelings for his future wife were matched by Emmeline's muted description of her feelings for him. Chapter Six of her autobiography describes in great detail her almost mystical feelings for her childhood mentor Mark Guy Pearse, and his involvement in the development of the Maison Esperance, and the search for holiday accommodation for the Esperance girls. But in contrast to Pearse – who was to become a great friend of Fred, and who conducted their wedding service – Emmeline describes her first meeting with Fred in 1899 in very unromantic terms. 'We were married in the Town Hall at Canning Town on October 2nd 1901,' wrote Emmeline in her autobiography.[17]

Fred, in his own autobiography, gave rather more detail:

> We decided on a somewhat unusual wedding... We wanted all to be there and 'all' included, in addition to our relatives and social and political fellow workers, the men of the Mansfield House Men's Club, the old ladies of the St Pancras workhouse, whom Emmeline was in the habit of visiting every week. The ceremony was performed by Percy Alden, Mark Guy Pearse and the Unitarian Minister of my family chapel... As the hall was not licensed for marriages we had the legal wedding in advance at St. Pancras Registry Office – 'short but binding' as the registrar said. We chartered a special train to Canning Town to bring the London guests. Everybody enjoyed the day, including, of course, the bride and groom. And people wrote afterwards recalling the 'sunny' day, which in fact had been overcast with cloud.[18]

Years before, when Emmeline was walking in the Alps an old lady had said to Emmeline's friend Marie:

"Never let that friend of yours marry!"
  "Why not?" asked Marie.
  "Because, my dear, she will never laugh like that again.
Never let her marry!"[19]

As it turned out Fred and Emmeline's marriage was full of laughter, friendship and shared endeavour, none more so than in their commitment to the suffragette cause, as we will see in the next chapter.

Emmeline had been very confused about sex as a child,[20] having been fobbed off with stories of babies arriving in the doctor's bag, or being found under a bush in the garden, and there has been some speculation that their childless marriage might have been celibate although there is some evidence of an early miscarriage.[21]

It is pointless, and prurient, to speculate about the intimate details of their marriage, but certainly their letters to each other (which flowed freely between them throughout their lives and were often sent daily, usually when one or other of them was abroad) are romantic in a rather courtly, sentimental way. They are peppered with endearments, but are certainly not earthy or passionate, as this letter of 1904 shows:

> Beloved
>   Such a scrubby little line I sent to greet ye in the morning. A rush of work, a great hurry to catch the train, but dear love to my own sweetheart… But O Patz your laddie thinks of you and wishes you a sweet time and then on Monday we meet again!
>   Arms around
>   Your own
>   Silly Billy[22]

Ten months later in, November 1904. Emmeline wrote to Fred from Egypt in almost mystical terms:

> Beloved. I scarcely know how to sit down and write to you tonight. My heart is too full. I could sit still for hours wrapped in a garment of joy. Every sense satisfied to the utmost…one's whole being seeped in sensation. Nothing has ever been the least bit like it – light and colour and wonder … My own darling Laddie, I hope that you are well and happy and that everything is going well. You are always in my heart. I often think how eager you were that I should come here.

More than 40 years later, on 28 March 1946, Fred wrote to Emmeline from the Viceroy's House in New Delhi:

> Dear old sweetheart. I hope you are enjoying your dear self. It will be a great delight to come back to you but is a long way off yet.
>   Your own precious love
>   Boy

And a week later, on April 7 1946, still in Delhi, Fred wrote:

> My own Darling
>   Another Sunday has come round – a fortnight since we arrived. Light, heat, colour, experience, endeavour, endless patience, endurance and my family motto "per ardua stabilis". My body is a perfect "brick". It has never wavered in its allegiance & has played the game magnificently. My spirit has not flagged. Your noble words written before I left, to the effect that in a measure you and I had already escaped from the wheel of life and death have come to me from time to time. Your love token bearing witness to our relationship to the central life is with me. It is of course much too early even to begin to think of the time when I shall be coming back. There are many rivers still to cross., many adventures still to undertake, many problems still to face. But these are all part of the great enterprise on which I have set out & which God willing I have to carry through to a successful issue.[23]

Emmeline and Fred have become one of those iconic twentieth century couples, alongside Sidney and Beatrice Webb and John and Barbara Hammond.[24] The Pethick-Lawrences were well-known for their political partnership, feminism and radicalism, but 'they were also renowned for the quality of their marriage and the freedom each partner enjoyed within it.'[25]

Unusually, they decided to keep separate bank accounts and to combine their names on marriage, so that instead of remaining individually Lawrence and Pethick (or Mr and Mrs Lawrence) they become, jointly and memorably, the Pethick-Lawrences (affectionately shortened to Pethick (for Fred) and Partsie (for Emmeline).[26] Although it was not uncommon to create double-barrelled names in the early twentieth century, the degree of independence they maintained was rare.

3. 'An extraordinary outbreak at home … of disorder on behalf of women'

Emmeline and Fred spent time after their marriage in 1901 travelling and, in what was to become a familiar pattern, they often did not travel together. At home, Emmeline continued her social work with the girls' club and the Esperance Girls, with her friend Mary Neal, while Fred edited his newspaper, the *Echo*. In 1904 Emmeline achieved 'the fulfilment of my desire' to visit Egypt,[1] and in 1905, after closing down the *Echo*, which had not been a success, he took Emmeline to South Africa, where she met politicians, and the writer Olive Schreiner. Along with other suffragettes, Emmeline was later to read in prison Olive Schreiner's visionary and prophetic book *Three Dreams in a Desert*.[2]

Both Emmeline and Fred would have known about the work for female suffrage of Millicent Fawcett and the constitutional suffragists, who had been campaigning assiduously, if with spectacular lack of success, since 1866. It was while Emmeline and Fred were in South Africa that a 'startling account reached us of an extraordinary outbreak at home of disorder on the part of women'.[3]

This turned out to be the incident at an election meeting in Manchester in 1905, at which a speech by Sir Edward Grey, the Liberal statesman, was interrupted by two women – the working class activist Annie Kenney (1878-1953) and Christabel Pankhurst – shouting 'Votes for Women'. They were subsequently arrested and sent to prison.

This was one of the first manifestations of Emmeline Pankhurst's suffragettes: the militant wing of the suffragist movement. Emmeline was very keen to meet these women and, as it happened, the repercussions of this incident were to dominate Emmeline and Fred's lives for the next six years.

After she returned to London in 1906, Emmeline had a visit from Sylvia Pankhurst, the second child of Mrs Pankhurst, encouraged by the Labour leader Keir Hardie, who tried to persuade Emmeline that she had the practical and useful skills which would allow her to develop a branch of the Women's Social and Political Union in London, as Mrs Pankhurst had done in Manchester. This first approach failed, as Emmeline Pethick-Lawrence was more involved in trying to define 'new ways of social living' than starting a new organisation. Annie Kenney was then sent to invite Emmeline to become the national treasurer of the WSPU. Emmeline initially 'had no fancy to be drawn into a small group of brave and reckless people … who were prepared to dash themselves against the oldest tradition of human civilisation as well as one of the strongest Governments of modern times.'[4]

But Annie Kenney recognised that Emmeline had the talents – and the temperament – to give the WSPU what it needed:

> Mrs Lawrence is not a woman who will play at work or work without method or from pure inspiration. She must see where she is going, where the road will lead and what obstacles there may be to block the path. She was the person we needed. Christabel, Mrs Pankhurst and I were too temperamental and purely intuitive. So Providence sent the right woman at the right time to help in turning the tiny vessel into a great liner.[5]

In time Annie Kenney's relationship with Emmeline was to become very emotional and caused some unease: '[I]t frightened me', wrote Teresa Billington. 'I saw in it something unbalanced and primitive and possibly dangerous to the movement.'[6]

But her initial misgivings led Emmeline to take her friend Mary Neal to the next meeting, held in Sylvia Pankhurst's home, and there, almost against her better judgment, Emmeline found herself drawn in:

> How it happened, I hardly know, but that evening with Mary Neal and myself we formed ourselves into a Central London Committee of the WSPU and I was formally requested to become the honorary treasurer. I consented to accept this on condition my old friend Alfred G Sayers, a chartered accountant, would accept the position of honorary auditor…
>
> It was by a very extraordinary sequence of incidents that I, who am not of a revolutionary temperament, was drawn into a revolutionary movement like the WSPU. The first thing that drew me to it was the story of the imprisonment of the two girls who had raised the suffrage issue at the memorable meeting in Manchester. Then I was touched by the appeal of Annie Kenney and made the

> promise to go to this pathetic little committee that talked
> so bravely of their plan to rouse London but seemed so
> helpless.[7]

When she investigated further, Emmeline found out that the WSPU had 'no office, no organization, no money – no postage stamps even'. Its honorary secretary – Sylvia Pankhurst – was distraught, and her financial situation was desperate. Emmeline realised that if anyone was to save the group it must be her: 'It was not without some dismay that it was borne upon me that somebody had to come to the help of this brave little group, and that the finger of fate pointed at me.'[8]

Emmeline Pethick-Lawrence may have inherited almost nothing in material terms from the WSPU when she took on this task, but she did inherit four very powerful women – Emmeline Pankhurst, her daughters Sylvia and Christabel, and Christabel's acolyte Annie Kenney – each with their own incredible strengths and skills. But none of them understood how organisations worked, and they had absolutely no idea of finance. As Emmeline Pethick-Lawrence said, 'Theirs was the guerrilla method of political warfare. It became my business to give their genius a solid foundation.'[9] In 1906 the office of the WSPU moved from Sylvia's home into the Pethick-Lawrences' flat at Clement's Inn, with Emmeline's secretary initially typing up the Union's letters.

Mrs Pankhurst and Annie Kenney are seated. Emmeline Pethick-Lawrence stands alongside. Their driver is the discreet and stalwart Mr Rapley.

Christabel Pankhurst also moved in to live there, once she had finished her law degree, and she stayed for six years. Emmeline found the 'many interests' which had been her initial excuse not to get too involved in the WSPU had to be set aside, and the Union increasingly dominated her life. Gradually Fred got drawn in also: paying bills, contributing his business enterprise and knowledge of finance, and building an organisation that became far from 'pathetic' but the wonder of the political world. 'The revolutionary side of the militant agitation was created and developed by the Pankhursts, the organic growth of the national organisation was fostered and directed by our union with them,' Emmeline later recalled.[10]

Fred followed Emmeline into the suffrage movement in 1906, and once there he gave himself, heart and soul to the cause. He then, as we shall see, went on to have a distinguished career in Labour politics and in India. Fred inherited his family wealth from the building trade, in part following the death of his brother Alfred in 1900. Until he got involved in Labour politics in the 1920s he did not have a steady profession and instead immersed himself in good causes such as the settlement movement, editing the *Echo* newspaper and later *Votes for Women*. Although Fred would probably not qualify as super-rich, he could afford to travel extensively and to run two residences, in London and the country, and to generously support a number of causes including, of course, suffrage.

In Fred's seminal work *Women's Fight for the Vote* (published by the Woman's Press in 1910, eight years before the partial vote was won and when it was still a 'campaign in progress'), he gave a very clear explanation of why women wanted, and needed, the vote:

> Women want the vote for two essential reasons: firstly, in order that they may play their part in the life of the nation and introduce their point of view, so long neglected, into the government of the country; and, secondly in order that their interests may be safeguarded.
>
> Women, it has been well said, 'excel in the care of all living things'. Women represent the human point of view. It was a woman (Florence Nightingale) who revolutionised the care of the sick upon the Battlefield. It was a woman (Elizabeth Fry) who was responsible for bringing into our mediaeval prison system such traces of humanity as it possesses today. It was a woman (Harriet Beecher Stowe) who, by her writing, contributed so largely to the abolition of slavery in… America.

VOTES FOR WOMEN.

Photo. by Gothàrd, Leeds.

Mrs. PETHICK LAWRENCE,

*Treasurer of the National Women's
Social and Political Union,
4, Clement's Inn, Strand, W.C.*

*Emmeline Pethick-Lawrence was both elegant and efficient – as treasurer and
organiser.*

> For men to imagine that they can get on better in the government and administration of the country without taking counsel of women, is an assumption equally arrogant and ridiculous with that of a father who should exclude the mother from any influence in the home or in the care of her infant children.[11]

Emmeline found her skills as a speaker increasingly used on behalf of the WSPU. The archives of one of the venues for suffragette meetings – the Royal Albert Hall – reveal that between 1908 and 1912 Emmeline was constantly on the platform at mass meetings as speaker or chairman, alongside the Pankhursts and other 'stars'.[12]

And Emmeline found herself increasingly involved in the action as well as the administration of the WSPU. In 1906 she helped to organise a delegation to the prime minister, Sir Henry Campbell-Bannerman, followed by a very well-attended rally – although it brought no result. In June of that year she was involved in an attempt to talk to Asquith, the Chancellor of the Exchequer and one of the arch-enemies of Votes for Women, at his home at 20 Cavendish Square, which resulted in several arrests and imprisonments. These were followed by the first celebrations of suffragettes' release from prison, which were to become such a feature of WSPU life.

The staff of the WSPU was expanding. Annie Kenney became the first London organiser, and Teresa Billington (1876-1964) and Mary Gawthorpe (1881-1973) joined the small inner group of organisers, alongside Charlotte Despard (1844-1939), a wealthy activist and sister of General Sir John French, who commanded the British army on the Western front from August 1914 onwards. Edith How Martyn (1875-1954) took over from Sylvia Pankhurst as joint honorary secretary, and Christabel became the WSPU's organising political secretary. Between them they formed a plan to attempt to speak in the chamber of the House of Commons, and in October 1906 ten of them, including Emmeline Pethick-Lawrence and Charlotte Despard, put the plan into practice. In her autobiography, Emmeline demonstrated both her intense courage and her intense nervousness both before and during the action – heart beating wildly, knees trembling, and losing her voice. She had just mustered the courage to speak in the chamber when she was summarily ejected, hustled through the lobby, and thrown out into the street. After a travesty of a trial, and her forcible removal from the police court,

> we had to wait some hours in the Cells before a prison van
> could be spared to take us to Holloway Prison, and as a
> consequence of the rough usage I felt very exhausted … I
> climbed into the van, my heart beating wildly. I shut my
> eyes and prayed that I might not lose self-control.
> Gradually my pulses beat less loudly and I began to
> breathe quietly.[13]

Emmeline learnt to cope with subsequent prison stays, but she
found this first one in 1906 extremely difficult, and it led to a nervous
breakdown, exhaustion and depression.[14] So worrying were her symp-
toms that her father and her husband were summoned to effect her
release on the grounds of ill-health. Once she had undertaken not to
take part in any militant action for six months, Fred took her straight to
Italy to recuperate while he took over the treasurership of the WSPU,
and with it 'a mass of business'. 'My imprisonment was the incident
that brought him finally to devote all his manifold powers to a cause
which needed the help that a trained mind like his could give,'
Emmeline later recalled.[15]

Alongside the heavy administrative burden, Fred also increasingly
took over the role of liaising between the police and arrested suffragettes (sometimes in their hundreds), and between the suffragettes and
their bewildered relations. He initiated a brilliant piece of fund-raising
by declaring that 'I am going to give £10 for the WSPU for every day of
my wife's sentence, and I should like to know who will follow my
example.'[16] In the event he not only raised a lot of money for campaign
organisers, but also sent a joke round the world in the form of a tag:

> Ten pounds a day
> He said he'd pay
> To keep this face
> In Holloway.

Two days after Emmeline's arrest, her father leant on Liberal
Members of Parliament to put all 'political prisoners' (those whose
offences were devoid of 'moral obliquity' [blame], and who could thus
be seen as prisoners of conscience) into the 'First Division'. Being held
in the First Division carried a number of privileges for incarcerated
women, such as being able to carry on their professions, and it definitely made prison a less onerous experience. The 'great-hearted'
Millicent Fawcett, despite her continued objection to militancy, gave
her support and organised a banquet at the Savoy Hotel to celebrate

Emmeline receives a bouquet of flowers from Jenny Baines and Flora Drummond, while Fred looks on.

with those prisoners who had been released early.[17]

Emmeline, meanwhile, was convalescing in Italy, feeling sad about a visit by her ailing father to see her there, and ashamed and humiliated by the 'crushing burden' of what she saw as her failure to cope with the trauma of imprisonment. Her spirits were not raised by a trip to Venice and northern Italy with the newly-released Sylvia Pankhurst. The wonder of the sights

> hurt me by their beauty. I longed to be fit to go back to London and take up my work there again... I resolved that I would dedicate the whole of the following year to the work that it remained open to me to do, and that I would overcome my nervous horror at being locked in dark and narrow places. I was able to carry out both these resolutions, for I went through five more imprisonments without undue suffering and never again was I to become the victim of my nerves. Indeed I subsequently experienced times of great mental peace and happiness in the solitude of the prison cell.[18]

Back in London in early 1907, there was a mass of suffrage activity on both the constitutional suffragist and the militant suffragette sides (both by those who, like Millicent Fawcett, believed in working within the law and those who increasingly did not). The term 'suffragette' had been coined by the *Daily Mail* and was at first intended to be belittling, but in the event the WSPU, and particularly Christabel Pankhurst, welcomed their new name. 'There was a spirit in it, a spring that we liked. "Suffragists" we had called ourselves until then, but that name lacked the positive note implied by "Suffragette"'.[19] The Women's Parliament in Caxton Hall, was organised by the WSPU at the time of the King's speech in February 1907 (described by Sylvia Pankhurst as a 'rallying ground for those who were to march up to the House of Commons to get themselves arrested').[20] The event spilled over into demonstrations in Parliament Square, and ended with the arrests of 54 women and two men. In March a woman suffrage bill was 'talked out', and a second Women's Parliament resulted in the arrests of 72 women, all of whom were imprisoned for six weeks.

Meanwhile the first annual report of the London Headquarters of the WSPU firmly established the main lines of WSPU policy, and there was a massive increase in activity, staff, premises, and revenue (from virtually nothing to £3,000 per year). All were to continue to grow further in the next five years.

But if everything was going spectacularly well on the external organisational front, there were within the organisation intimations of disquiet. Discussions about the need for a constitution, and for internal democracy, were vehemently rejected by Emmeline and Christabel Pankhurst (who were becoming increasingly autocratic). There was much debate about the WSPU's leadership, with a move by Charlotte Despard, Edith How Martyn and Teresa Billington-Greig to replace the leadership of Emmeline and Christabel Pankhurst. In the event, Despard led her colleagues into a new organisation, the Women's Freedom League (WFL), in a move that came to be known as 'The Split', but the WSPU continued to gather immense momentum. It became ultimately so strong that 'it left its mark on the history of the country'.[21]

While the WSPU was being reorganised, and all its members were asked to pledge not to support any political party until Votes for Women were won, Emmeline Pethick-Lawrence joined its new

Opposite: Another elegant picture of Emmeline soon after she became co-editor, with Fred, of Votes for Women *in 1907.*

Above: Two front covers of Votes for Women. *(Opposite) Its success can be seen by how busy the WSPU despatch department was [Museum of London]*

national committee, although this did not meet until 1912. Meanwhile, Mrs Pankhurst, who 'disliked administrative detail'[22] was set free from all office administration, giving her time to tour the country, 'addressing large meetings', and winning over supporters everywhere. While she did so the office's finances and business were run, both from Clement's Inn and Surrey, by Emmeline, Fred and Christabel, and helped by an efficient and enthusiastic staff, both paid and unpaid. They settled the immediate policy of the union, while branches were left free to adapt their methods to local conditions. Emmeline wrote that 'an atmosphere of comradeship, confidence and happiness was maintained between members and organisers and the next five years witnessed extraordinary developments,'[23] including the launch of Fred and Emmeline's newspaper *Votes for Women* in October 1907. This was set up to great acclaim, and they became its co-editors.

The phrase 'Votes for Women' had long been the battle-cry of the WSPU, and it now became the title of their newspaper, published by the St Clement's Press. It was first published in 1907 monthly but it became weekly in April 1908, and by 1910 its circulation had risen to 30,000. When the split came between the Pankhursts and the Pethick-

Lawrences, Emmeline and Fred retained the ownership and editorship of *Votes for Women* and in due course they took it with them into their new organisation, the United Suffragists.

During the next five months, over the winter of 1907-08, there was a massive mobilisation of WSPU members under the guise of an intensive educational campaign, with members attending mass meetings (addressed by both Mrs Pankhurst and Christabel), marching, protesting and processing. In February 1908, when the King's Speech once more made no mention of Votes for Women, a three-day gathering of women convened at Caxton Hall. Two deputations to the prime minister were turned back as being more than the ten people permitted by an old statute dating back to the days of Charles I, and fifty women were arrested, tried (with the aptly-named Mr Muskett prosecuting), and sentenced to six weeks in the second division, which meant their political status – with corresponding privileges – was not recognised.

Mrs Pankhurst then descended from a by-election in South Leeds, where she had been campaigning for votes for women, and offered to carry the resolution with no more than ten people. This was no more successful, and Emmeline Pankhurst and her deputation were sentenced to six weeks in Holloway. A week of 'self-denial' – a sponsored giving up of luxuries – was instituted, which raised around £7,000. A second annual report was prepared (showing yet more progress on all fronts), and elaborate preparations were made for a mass meeting in the Royal Albert Hall on 19 March 1908, which was claimed to be the largest gathering of women ever under one roof. At the last minute

Emmeline Pankhurst was undoubtedly a first class campaigner, but her treatment of the Pethick-Lawrences was more problematic.

Emmeline Pankhurst was released from jail, and she was greeted onto the platform of the Royal Albert Hall to huge acclaim.

1908 was an important time for the suffrage movement. 'Not a month, not a week even, passed unmarked, by outstanding and thrilling events'.'[25] On 20 March 1908 those leaving Holloway were greeted by a celebratory breakfast at the Wharncliffe Rooms. They were then driven to the Peckham by-election which was one of several Liberal electoral defeats (including Winston Churchill's in North-West Manchester, a few weeks later) that were attributed to the suffragettes. In Peckham the government was defeated by a swing of nearly 5,000 votes.

In the early summer the Union's activities were concentrated on mass, record-breaking demonstrations in Hyde Park where Fred, as honorary organiser-in chief, brought together at least a quarter of a million people on 21 June. The event was on a gigantic scale which also involved 64 trains to get people there, and seven meticulously organised processions accompanied by forty bands, with 'General' Flora Drummond (1878-1969) – a distinguished suffragette who liked to wear military garb – being very prominent.

Emmeline made elaborate claims for this event. 'It is no exaggeration to say that never before had such numbers of people been gathered in one spot in the history of the world.'[26] The event passed without accident, aided by the fact that Fred had ordered considerable numbers of the iron railings in the park to be removed in order to avoid injury. The response by the press was astonishingly positive: newspapers reported that the rally was 'Daringly conceived, splendidly stage-managed and successfully carried out' and that 'This movement has done in less than three years what all the gentle persuasion of a generation had failed to effect.'[27]

The rally was also astonishingly beautiful with all the suffragettes in their purple, white and green outfits. This was again thanks to Emmeline, who contributed not only her organisational and financial skills – and her oratory – to the cause, but also her creativity. Emmeline was a great admirer of William Morris, and it was she who first conceived this combination of colours. In her weekly newspaper *Votes for Women*, she explained the symbolism:

> Purple as everyone knows is the royal colour. It stands for the royal blood that flows in the veins of every suffragette, the instinct of freedom and dignity … white stands for purity in private and public life … green is the colour of hope and the emblem of spring.[28]

Emmeline was keenly aware of the impact that colour-coded symbolism could have on the public, and *Votes for Women* encouraged suffragettes to display the colours at all times – and, of course, especially on marches and demonstrations:

> The colours enable us to make that appeal to the eye which is so irresistible. The result of our processions is that movement becomes identified in the mind of the onlooker with colour, gay sound, movement, [and] beauty.[29]

The suffragette colours soon caught on like wildfire and they began to appear everywhere, from the dresses of women processing in the street or at mass meetings, to a huge range of merchandise – jewellery, scarves, motor veils, cups and saucers. In the 18 June 1908 issue of *Votes for Women*, Emmeline exhorted all WSPU members to wear the Suffragette colours for the Women's Sunday Procession and Hyde Park demonstration on 21st June. She notes that 'General' Drummond had specifically mentioned that 'everyone who wants to go should wear our special scarf'.

Two suffragettes carried militancy to its next level by breaking windows in Downing Street, and were sentenced to two months imprisonment. The press responded with a new note of respect. It was not only the London and provincial press that presented these views, but the press of the whole Western world followed suit. Women's suffrage, for the first time in its history, had become 'news'. Emmeline felt ecstatic about the feeling of solidarity which women in the movement felt towards each other, and their cause:

> Women of the upper middle and working classes realized a new comradeship with each other. Neither class, nor wealth, nor education counted any more, only devotion to the common ideal. No longer did women feel loneliness or isolation or inhibition. There was a heightening of the values of life for us all.[30]

During the month of July one demonstration followed another: Clapham Common, Nottingham Forest, Manchester, Leeds – with crowds of 20,000-100,000. Every few days witnessed a mass meeting in some part of England, Wales and Scotland. Emmeline noted that in the press Votes for Women was the only cause.'

On 23 July 1908 Christabel wrote about the importance of deeds rather than just words (one of the mantras of the movement) in *Votes For Women*. On July 29 there were scandalous reports of women trying to interrupt – both loudly and aggressively – Lloyd George, who was then chancellor of the Exchequer, at a meeting of the International Peace Congress at the Queen's Hall. Come August, the wealthier suffragettes were scattered to the moors, the rivers and the beaches on their holidays. Meanwhile Emmeline met Lady Constance Lytton at the Green Lady Hostel, the holiday house on the Sussex coast that had been set up for the girls of the Esperance Guild and Club.

In September 1908 there was a by-election in Newcastle which was catastrophic for the Liberals: having had a previous majority of over 6,000, they lost to the Conservatives by more than 2,000 votes. Involvement in by-elections thus became an instrument in the WSPU's campaign against the Liberal Government. Mrs Pankhurst, who had been very prominent in the by-election and thus instrumental in the Liberals' defeat, appealed to the Prime Minister for a third reading for a Suffrage Bill proposed by a Liberal MP, Henry Yorke

Annie Kenney, Lady Constance Lytton and Emmeline in the country at the Green Lady Hostel. Emmeline is planting a tree

Emmeline Pethick-Lawrence and Christabel Pankhurst on the campaign trail.

Stanger. This was declined, but there was huge popular support for the bill, led by the suffragettes, and on 11 October a mass meeting was held in Trafalgar Square under the banner 'Votes for Women! Come to the House of Commons on October 13 at 7.30 pm.' This was subsequently misreported as a call to 'rush' the House of Commons chamber, not just to gather outside the Palace of Westminster, and Mrs Pankhurst, Christabel and 'General' Drummond were summoned to attend the police court at Bow Street. They laid low in Emmeline's private flat (given to her by Fred on their first wedding anniversary), which was hidden away in Clement's Inn, but they emerged in time to submit themselves to the court at 6.00pm as promised.

Emmeline Pethick-Lawrence now found herself due to address a meeting at Caxton Hall, as the only speaker who had not been imprisoned, and she faced the challenge of a hall full of male medical students – most of them opposed to votes for women – who she managed to persuade to leave before WSPU supporters streamed in. 'This occasion was one of those moments when I knew that our movement was guided by spiritual powers. It was no power of my own that prevailed,' she later wrote.[31]

Eleven women volunteered to take Stanger's bill to the House of Commons, while Parliament Square was flooded with police. An omnibus full of suffragettes was greeted with cheers by an 'extraordinarily friendly' crowd. A Mrs Travers Simmons managed to enter the chamber of the House of Commons but she was thrown out, arrested in the Members' Lobby, and subsequently released.

The police appeared to have been told to exhaust the suffragettes rather than arrest them. The suffragettes definitely had the support of the crowd, but at the end of the day 24 women and 12 men were arrested, and they were all sentenced to three weeks' imprisonment. Meanwhile Mrs Pankhurst, Christabel and 'General' Drummond, all of them detained in Bow Street, were much comforted by bedding and food sent in from the Savoy Hotel by a well-wisher MP.

Lady Constance Lytton had first met Emmeline at the Green Lady Hostel during a holiday with the Esperance girls in September 1908. At that time she had shown absolutely no interest in Votes for Women, and had not realised at first that her holiday companions were suffragettes. But Lytton was now a transformed person, shuttling between Clement's Inn, the House of Commons, and the police court on Bow Street in a desperate attempt to mitigate the sentences that were meted out to the women. 'All these experiences had changed her from an interested onlooker into a red-hot militant', claimed Emmeline.[32]

Christabel Pankhurst, armed with legal knowledge, having graduated with her law degree, now decided to subpoena two senior Liberal MPs – the Chancellor of the Exchequer David Lloyd George, and the Home Secretary Herbert Gladstone[33] as witnesses, since they had been present at the demonstrations. Her aim was to prove that the crowd on 13 October was an orderly one. Christabel appeared in the dock, alongside her mother and 'General' Drummond, in 'a white dress with a sash of purple and green, looking like a flower in that dingy court.'[34] She only had limited time for cross-examination, since the witnesses had 'important business' to attend to, but she managed to get both Lloyd George and Herbert Gladstone to concede that they had not felt under any personal threat from the demonstrators (and, in the Chancellor's case, there had been no threat to his six-year-old daughter, who had been with him). In spite of brilliant closing speeches from Mrs Pankhurst and Christabel (Mrs Pankhurst's was so moving that it reduced even hardened police officers to tears)[35] not to mention the publicity which Emmeline described as like 'a suffrage meeting attended by millions', the verdict was brutal. The prisoners were to be bound over to keep the peace for twelve months, and in default the two elder ones were to be kept in prison for three months and the younger

*Lloyd George in the witness box at a suffragette trial: cross-examined by
Christabel, he had to admit that at no time did he or his family feel threatened*

for ten weeks – a verdict which had a 'dread effect on all'.[36] Christabel
had a particularly severe response to the threat of imprisonment. But at
the same time she was becoming the icon, the 'Portia' of the press,
whose idealistic buoyancy, youth and charm contrasted very painfully
with 'the middle-age and no illusions left' Lloyd George.[37]

Two or three days after the end of the trial, Emmeline was in the
Royal Albert Hall again, chairing a very oversubscribed meeting to
raise funds for the WSPU. The atmosphere was joyful, and 'the excite-

ment and enthusiasm were intoxicating,'[38] with suffragettes in purple, white and green collecting money, and with Fred on hand to mark up on a blackboard the donations made. In the end nearly £3,000 was raised in cash, jewellery and personal effects: another testament to Emmeline's fund-raising skills.

Emmeline was also becoming renowned as a writer of trenchant pamphlets on the WSPU's behalf. In *Why I went to Prison?* she answered her own question 'Because the approved way to the freedom of women lies through prison gates'. Noting 'the helplessness of women, who are politically bound and gagged', she insists that 'the greatest hope for humanity is the release of the women's soul and mind and body'.[39]

Looking back decades later, Emmeline wondered whether the pace of the movement at this point was too fast, with one demonstration relentlessly following another. The temperature of the movement was at white heat, and cabinet ministers needed the support of large numbers of police when facing the suffragettes. The WSPU was then presented with a dilemma when Lloyd George agreed to speak about women's suffrage on the platform of the Women's Liberal Federation in the Royal Albert Hall in November 1908. In their view Lloyd George had two alternative courses of action: either take full responsibility to grant women the vote, or lay down this responsibility by resigning. Anything less would mean the WSPU would re-adopt its policy of heckling. He did neither, so Emmeline published an article entitled 'Political Flirtation' in which she pointed out that the Chancellor of the Exchequer was playing the part of the political philanderer. When the speech came the heckling was very severe: 'Women were not only thrown out of the meeting, which they accepted as a natural consequence but they were assaulted and beaten up in a disgraceful manner.'[40]

After another meeting in Leeds, a Mrs Baines was tried for unlawful assembly and defended in court by Fred, who was a qualified barrister, if not a very experienced one. Mrs Baines was found guilty and committed to prison for six weeks. On a more cheerful note, Christabel Pankhurst and her mother were released from prison together in December 1908. In a red-letter day for the WSPU, the 'beloved founders' were welcomed to breakfast at the Inns of Court Hotel by 500 people, and gave stirring speeches. Early in 1909 the WSPU's third annual report showed even greater progress than the previous two – with income up from £6000 to £18,000. The Women's Press (which published suffragette leaflets) was doing well, and the paper *Votes for Women*, with its circulation of nearly 30,000 and large advertising revenue, spoke with authority on all aspects of the suffrage movement. 'But what gave the paper its unique success was the enthusiastic support of the rank and file who stood in all weathers at street corners to sell it to all comers,' Emmeline later explained.[41]

The WSPU's head office in Clement's Inn now consisted of 19 rooms, with paid staff increased from 32 to 75, and hundreds of volunteers. The WSPU had participated in, and influenced the outcome of, 19 by-elections as an active lobby group, conducted many mass meetings around the country. In a unique bit of fundraising on Emmeline's behalf, this was all paid for by 'propaganda meetings', at which every seat was paid for. Emmeline expressed admiration in her autobiography for Millicent Fawcett, the original non-militant suffragist, and acknowledged the other suffrage organisations which were springing up, such as the Actresses' Franchise League, the League of Women Writers, the Graduates' University Suffrage Society and the Men's League for Woman Suffrage. She thought that the women's movement went far beyond the vote:

> It meant also to women the discovery of their wealth of spiritual sympathy, lotyalty and the affection that could be formed in intercourse, friendship and companionship with one another … the suffrage campaign was our Eton and Oxford, our regiment, our ship, our cricket match.[42]

The movement broke down class barriers ('marching between a dowager duchess and a laundry maid'), developed personal friendships, led to the quickening of intelligence and wit, and a 'quickening of the whole emotional life.[43] A speech by Christabel underlined the transformational quality of the movement, particularly to the young: 'The young people find a world entirely contrary to our own. We mean to mould a new world to our will!' At the same time, many distinguished and first-rate speakers – the actors Sir Johnston Forbes-Robertson and Granville Barker, and the actress, playwright and suffragette Elizabeth Robins – shared a WSPU platform in the Queen's Hall on 11 February 1909 and it was inspiring to have so many of the finest minds not only in sympathy but in active participation.'[44]

> [t]he unknown members received the worst of the hard knocks and met them with the greatest heroism, while the leaders were rewarded not only with the devotion of their followers but with the acclaim of a large section of the population.[45]

Emmeline was imprisoned, in all, six times for suffragette offences. In her memoir she described in detail the horrors both of the admission process to prison (when women were normally issued with filthy prison clothes), and of the hospital ward in Holloway where she spent some time. But by the time her sentence in 1909 ended, she had lost her fear of confined spaces 'that had haunted me all my life', that made her previous visit to prison so terrifying. She 'realised that the locked cell could become as conducive to meditation as the mountain cave to the ascetic' and developed 'a prison mood of happiness'. And she was sustained by her commitment to the cause, writing to the WSPU on 26 March:

> Oh to see our flag again! To salute the colours! My eyes yearn for them. I comfort myself with the thought that my prison dress is green, my prison cap is white...
> Would that my apron were purple. My library card is

Chaining oneself to railings became a favourite tactic.

A typical breakfast in the Queen's Hall celebrating the release of suffragette prisoners.

faintly purplish! But one lives on small things in Holloway. And how one's perceptions and appreciations are intensified, How one learns the meanings and the values of the ordinary blessings and beauties of life which one is so apt to take for granted. Colour, music, sun and stars, and above all human friendship and social intercourse.[46]

On her release from Holloway she was welcomed by 600 people for breakfast in the Wharncliffe Rooms and presented with a motor car in the suffragette colours (the car was not for Emmeline's exclusive use: it was subsequently used by the WSPU as a whole). Emmeline had been accompanied into prison by Lady Constance Lytton, who had a passionate interest in prison conditions which she chronicled in her book *Prison and Prisoners*. The reform of prison was as much Lytton's agenda as anything to do with *Votes for Women* was, and she regarded her stay in prison as essential empathetic research for improving prison conditions. Lytton was hugely comforted to find Emmeline in prison with her but dismayed by the conditions, particularly for 'ordinary prisoners':

> Beside the sink there was tiny sash window about the level of my head. When this was open I could catch sight of the yard where remand prisoners exercised. I was surprised to see that many of them wore prison dress. This meant either that they had been made to change their clothes, or that remand and convicted prisoners were exercising together). Seeing a great number of prisoners in a group was a most depressing sight. They were packed quite close, touching each other as they went round the narrow asphalt path in single file. They – nearly all of them – looked ill. Their faces wore an air of extreme dejection; the lifeless, listless way they walked... Anxiety, suffering, bitterness, and a harrowing tale of want or degradation.[47]

Lytton expressed irritation that she was apparently receiving preferential treatment (better accommodation, more health checks and better food) because of who she was and the fact her father had been Viceroy of India: 'The action of the authorities made no pretence at inflexible, even-handed justice, and the partiality shown was all on behalf of the prisoner who needed it least'.[48] Lytton found out how true this was when she was subsequently imprisoned, and forcibly fed, while masquerading as a working-class woman.

The day after her release from Holloway in 1909 Emmeline joined, with her young niece Freda Budgett, an imposing procession from west London to the Aldwych, in a carriage with four fine grey horses and behind the banner 'Now May Hope Bear Sweet Fruition', and a woman dressed as Joan of Arc (an icon to the suffragettes) on horseback. And in May 1909 she was very involved in the WSPU's Gala Exhibition at the Princes Skating Rink, Knightsbridge, which was a whirl of activity that raised £5,000 from the public. The gala included performances by the Actresses' Franchise League, and an art exhibition coordinated by Sylvia Pankhurst around the theme 'They Who Sow In Tears Shall Reap In Joy'.

But the usual business of the Union continued alongside these festivities. Throughout the country the hard slog of campaigning went on. There were various encounters between cabinet ministers and members of the WSPU, with varying degrees of hostility. And there was the famous incident in 1909, at an honorary degree giving in Liverpool, at which a local organiser, Mary Phillips, managed to hide herself for 24 hours under the platform before the ceremony began. To everyone's astonishment, her disembodied cry 'Votes for Women', and complaints about the recent imprisonment of a local woman, were audible around the hall without the speaker, the Liberal politician Mr Birrell, or anyone else knowing where they came from.[49]

Meanwhile, in spite of accusations to the contrary, no suffragette or supporter was ever convicted of assault on the person. Rather the reverse: many suffragettes were badly injured by police and men in the crowd at meetings. Lord Lytton (Constance's brother), speaking on a WSPU platform at the Queen's Hall in June 1909, said that militancy was a matter of the 'utmost regret', but declared his 'profound conviction that after so many years spent in peaceful persuasion without results, no other methods were open to women who were serious and determined'.

The treatment of the suffragettes in prison was debated in parliament in June, and in the same month, Wallace Dunlop[50] stamped in violet ink, on the wall of St Stephens Hall in the House of Commons, the words,

WOMEN'S DEPUTATION
JUNE 29
BILL OF RIGHTS
IT IS THE RIGHT OF THE SUBJECTS TO PETITION THE KING – AND ALL
COMMITMENTS AND PROSECUTIONS FOR SUCH PETITIONING IS
ILLEGAL[51]

Dunlop was promptly arrested for this 'latest suffragist outrage'.

On 29 June 1909, Mrs Pankhurst led an advertised deputation of women from Caxton Hall to the House of Commons: 'The crowd received her with overwhelming enthusiasm… It was the welcome we read of citizens giving to a queen who had saved them…' On the steps of St Stephen's Hall Mrs Pankhurst was greeted by an Inspector Jarvis, who handed her a letter from the Prime Minister denying her an interview. In order to effect an immediate arrest, and avoid aggressive jostling for herself and her elderly companions, Mrs Pankhurst struck Inspector Jarvis lightly on the cheek, and was arrested. In 1936 Inspector Jarvis (who was very popular with the WSPU because of his relative leniency towards them) was invited to sit on the top table at a celebration dinner for Emmeline Pethick-Lawrence, at which he gave a gracious little speech saying that he always knew the suffragettes should win the vote 'because when women had made up their minds they always got what they wanted'.[52]

Mrs Pankhurst and Christabel dressed in prison garb as part of the Prisons to Citizenship Pageant.

Inside the House, on 29 June 1909, Keir Hardie urged that the deputation from the WSPU should be received. Nearby, the first of many
window-breaking incidents occurred at the Home Office, where
stones were wrapped in paper and tied up in string, knocked against the
glass and dropped through the hole, to avoid the small risk of injury to
any person in the room. This was in fact the first truly 'militant' act in
the campaign:

> the initiative was taken by members of the rank and file,
> and afterwards accepted by the leaders of the movement,
> because they realized that it was impossible to restrain any
> longer the more determined of their colleagues.[53]

Meanwhile the WSPU was now getting a good press – and on the
whole good treatment from the police. On 29 June 1909 108 women
were arrested and Evelina Haverfield and Emmeline Pankhurst were
put in the dock, with Mr Muskett again acting on the Government's
behalf. Pending the hearing of the case, all of the 108 were freed, and
none of them ever served their full sentence. Subsequently re-arrested,
Wallace Dunlop tried to achieve the status of a political prisoner but
instead, like many others, she subjected herself to a hunger strike
which at this stage was a route out of prison.

Meanwhile men were becoming more active in the movement and
were setting up the Men's Political Union (MPU), alongside the
Men's League for Women's Suffrage. The MPU's members could
attend meetings attended by cabinet ministers (from which women
were excluded), and subject them to determined questioning. With
great courage, many MPU members experienced brutal handling at
these meetings. More than a dozen of them had to receive medical
treatment for broken bones. Emmeline was always keen to emphasise
that the movement was hugely enhanced by the presence of men, and
that while it was certainly anti-Government it was never anti-men.

Meanwhile, suffragettes in prison were subjecting themselves to a
variety of strikes – hunger strikes, refusal to wear regulation prison
dress. 'Many had stories to tell, when they were released, of punishment and handcuffs and other tortures' and 'there was no holding
from breaking back the spirit of revolt'. The desire for sacrifice became
a passion that could not be held in leash, wrote Emmeline:

> Let no one think of the hunger-strike as a light matter:
> 'When carrying out the hunger-strike in prison,' wrote a
> released prisoner 'one is made to feel that the probability

of being allowed to die is a strong one. I felt it right up to
the moment of my release and felt that to go and die
would be easy.[54]

Other punishments included solitary confinement, handcuffing for
long periods, and being placed in straitjackets for their refusal to wear
prison dress. Owing to these conditions in prison, many suffragettes
had to be carefully nursed back to normal health after their release. But
far from breaking their spirit, their poor treatment incited them to
deeds of great daring in pursuance of the campaign. On September 17
the Prime Minster made a trip to give a political speech in Birmingham. It was as if the city was under siege, with barricades everywhere.

Who could guess that all these precautions were taken to
prevent one unhappy obstinate old man being forced to
grant an interview to a small (but determined) band of
women?[55]

The day ended with multiple arrests.
In *Votes for Women* Emmeline wrote at this time:

Women in direct opposition to their instinct, tradition and
normal character have been forced into revolutionary
action in defence of their rights and liberties, and for this
the Government is responsible, not the women... The
Government in forcing this issue upon us has calculated
from the outset on women's hatred of violence, as the
guarantee of success for its policy of repression, but it has
discounted the determination of women never to abandon this legitimate fight for a cause that is dearer to them
than life.[56]

Action instigated by the government against the hunger strike had
been hardening, and it now solidified into full-scale forcible feeding
(which involved introducing a tube down the nostrils or the throat,
causing intense suffering, and often physical damage). In the month of
September 1909 'the militant suffrage movement... hurled itself forward with terrific and overpowering momentum:

During the first three or four years, in spite of rough handling by Liberal stewards, in spite of batterings in
Parliament Square, in spite of imprisonments, the spirit of

laughter and adventure, the spirit of youth had been dominant amongst us. But when the Government decided to
counter hunger-strike with forcible feeding, then every
militant suffragette came face to face with acute and
almost intolerable suffering and the temper of the movement became one of fierce determination to count no cost
and to stake life itself in the struggle.[57]

As news of forcible feeding reached the public domain, there was a
huge outcry in a memorial signed by 116 doctors of all persuasions,
one of whom (Hugh Tenton) railed against 'this absolutely beastly and

A graphic depiction of the horrors of forcible feeding appeared in the Suffragette,
*the paper that became the official voice of the WSPU after the Pethick-
Lawrences left (with* Votes for Women*) in 1912. The* Suffragette *became
the patriotic publication Britannia in 1914, and ceased publication in December
1918. The* Suffragette *never reached the same circulation achieved by* Votes
for Women

revolting procedure'.[58] An all-party deputation of MPs, led by Keir Hardie, went to the Home Secretary, Herbert Gladstone. 'The response to all the outcries was only one rejoinder:

> 'The suffragettes will not stay in prison, they fight their way out by adopting the hunger-strike'. …We must either let then die or feed then by force. Our (the WSPU) reply …was 'Give women the Vote (the majority of your party are already pledged to women's franchise) and the problem will be solved.'[59]

Reading through the pages of *Votes for Women*, it is clear that Emmeline was amazed by the suffering and the courage of many women. Of the many acts of heroism, the twelve suffragettes arrested in Newcastle stand out. Each of them put a stone through a window of the Liberal Club, the Post Office or another public building, as a witness to the fact that they did not fear the gag, the tube, or any other form of torture. Emmeline was particularly anxious about two of the suffragettes: her friend Constance Lytton and her own sister, Dorothy Pethick. In the event they both escaped forcible feeding on health grounds through 'a piece of class snobbery', which made Constance Lytton determined to go to prison next time disguised as a working-class girl so she could share what these 'unknown' women endured.[60] The case of Mary Leigh (who had been one of the first to break windows in Downing Street), with her 'calm and quiet demeanour' and moral strength, illustrated how a prisoner lost her normal human rights during incarceration.

In December 1909 two working-class women 'unknown to the public' – Selina Martin and Leslie Hall – were arrested for throwing a missile into the Prime Minister's empty car (which was undamaged) in Liverpool. They were treated exceptionally savagely, being handcuffed, frog-marched and forcibly fed in punishment cells.[61] This prompted Constance Lytton to adopt the alias of 'Jane Warton', a seamstress. 'Jane Warton' was arrested for subversive behaviour and sent to Walton jail in Liverpool, where 'without my heart being tested or my pulse felt, I was fed twice a day through the mouth by means of the stomach tube (the mouth forced and kept open by a gag). The operation,

> invariably induced vomiting. In spite of first-hand accounts I had heard of this process, the reality surpassed all that I had anticipated – it was a living nightmare of pain, horror and revolting degradation. The anguish and,

A WSPU delegation at 10 Downing Street, one of many futile attempts to lobby the government.

> effort of retching while the tube is forcibly pressed back
> into the stomach and the natural writhings of the body
> defy all descriptions… Except in the way of clenching my
> teeth, I offered no resistance.[62]

On her release, her story electrified the public. When news got out that the daughter of the first Earl of Lytton, and a former Viceroy of India, had been tortured in this way (causing lasting damage to her arm and voice), a major controversy ensued between the Home Office and the present Lord Lytton, her brother. The new Home Secretary, Winston Churchill, formulated new rules whereby offenders who had not been convicted of 'moral turpitude' were exempted from some forms of prison discipline such as prison dress, had more rights of association in work and exercise, and were allowed more frequent exchange of letters and visits (this was not quite the status of political prisoners, but it did prove a more effective way of dealing with the hunger-strikers than forcible feeding).

In 1909 Henry Brailsford, a left-wing journalist, quietly gathered together a Parliamentary Conciliation Committee, and in June it announced its decision to promote a 'Conciliation Bill' to give votes to women householders and occupiers of business premises with a rate-able value of £10. It was not what the WSPU had been fighting for, but it had wide-ranging support, and the WSPU declared a truce from militancy, very much with Emmeline Pethick-Lawrence's support. The Bill was published in April 1910 as a private member's bill. Although it attained a majority, no further time was given to the Bill and at the end of July 1910 Parliament was prorogued until November, ahead of a general election in December 1910.

There was no mention of women's suffrage in the Liberal manifesto ahead of the election, and on 18 November Emmeline presided over a 'Parliament of Women' at Caxton Hall, made up of suffragists as well as suffragettes – and with women from as far away as America and Australia. This despatched 400 women to the House of Commons in groups of no more than 13 each. The first group, the official delegation, included Emmeline Pankhurst. Dr Elizabeth Garrett Anderson, Mrs Anne Cobden Sanderson[63] and Princess Duleep-Singh.[64] The prime minister Herbert Asquith refused to receive this delegation, and he packed Parliament Square with policemen who were extremely hostile to the suffragette cause. This led to extreme violence. In what became known as Black Friday, the *Western Times* reported that as they reached Westminster Abbey:

Here, however, a band of roughs offered obstacles to further progress, roughly jostling the women, while they
jeered and yelled with delight at their discomfiture.
Undaunted the ladies persevered, and though roughly
handled in the melee, presently joined forces with the
banner-bearers outside St. Stephen's entrance. This was
the signal for renewed hustling of a shameful character.
The banners were torn down and trampled in the grass to
the accompaniment of rude taunts, but headway was still
made, till the Suffragettes at last, gaining St, Stephen's
entrance, found the way barred by adamantine police.
The women waited patiently in the hope an interview
would be granted.[65]

It wasn't. Asquith had no intention of meeting the protestors, and
the violence intensified:

As the women tried to push forwards, they were kicked,
punched, pinched and had knees – or in some cases grop-
ing hands – thrust between their thighs. Police grabbed
women's hands and bent back their thumbs or fingers,
twisted their wrists and deliberately shoved the women
into the way of oncoming vehicles and crowds. One of
the most widespread methods of assault was for police to
grab women by the chest and twist their breasts agoniz-
ingly, It was not only the police who molested the
women: a mob of male anti-suffrage protestors joined in
and the police did nothing to stop them assaulting the
women. One woman later reported back to the WSPU
that when she had told a policeman he was assaulting her,
he had replied maliciously that he was allowed to 'grip
you wherever I like today', which led to the suspicion that
the police had been told to use sexual violence as a form of
crowd control.[66]

Fifty women were injured, and two subsequently died of heart
attacks. In a report presented to the Conciliation Committee by Jessie
Murray and Henry Brailsford, there were six categories of abuse:
Unnecessary violence; Methods of torture, i.e. bending thumbs back-
wards, twisting arms, pinching, gripping the throat and forcing back
with violence, forcing fingers up nostrils, and so on; Acts of
Indecency; After effects; State of mind of police; Plain-clothes men.

An aerial view of the Prison to Citizenship Pageant June 1911. The procession took place a week before the coronation of Edward VII, and was designed to be a patriotic gesture in the hope of winning the king's support. Sadly, the king showed no support whatsoever.

The Home Office refused to conduct an inquiry into "Black Friday", despite much public demand for one. Emmeline wondered whether the Government was deliberately pushing women towards more violent methods of protest, in the hope of weaning public support away from them.

The position of the WSPU had been strengthened by the general election of December 1910, in which they played a prominent part, and in which the Liberals lost ten seats they had held in the last Parliament. By the time of the WSPU's annual report of February 1911, the union had grown hugely in financial terms, in the size of its premises, and in the number of both paid staff (who now numbered 110) and volunteers. Indeed, the position of the women's suffrage campaign at the beginning of 1911 was better than it had ever been.

The new Parliament met in February 1911 with a redrafted Conciliation Bill which was 'read' with wide party support. The press were equally supportive: the *Daily News* wrote 'If the House is refused the time necessary for the complete disposal of the Bill, then both the liberties and the credit of the House will suffer even more seriously'.[67] 'All the stars seemed to be in our favour. And a week after the attainment of the large majority in the House of Lords. the Mayor of Dublin arrived on an official visit to present a petition which ended with these words 'Your petitioners therefore pray that the Bill to confer the Parliamentary franchise on women may be passed through your honourable House during the present session of Parliament'.[68] That same evening, in honour of the Lord Mayor, all the leaders of the various suffrage groups – including Millicent Fawcett and Charlotte Despard – came together for a celebration gathering, in the Connaught Rooms.

The suffrage barometer fell when it was stated that Parliament could give no further time to the bill in 1911, but it rose when there was a definite pledge that time would be made available in 1912. Christabel, writing in *Votes for Women*, showed extreme optimism 'and did, in the anticipation of victory, not slacken our efforts to bring the whole country into line'.[69] Her optimism was echoed in many other newspapers, and the WSPU continued to hold about 200 indoor and outdoor meetings a week. No political reform movement had, it was claimed, ever won such widespread public support.

Then, on 17 June, came the largest suffrage procession ever: over 40,000 women converged on the Royal Albert Hall, where they were greeted with great accolades by the press. Emmeline Pethick-Lawrence was at the front of the procession:

> As I walked amongst others at the head of the procession, I was able, on reaching our destination… to watch the advance of that great army marching five abreast. It was all deeply moving. To me, naturally enough, the most significant and beautiful part of the pageant was the contingent of those who had been in prison. They marched in white, a thousand strong, each one carrying a small silver pennant, and in their midst was borne a great banner depicting a symbolic woman with a chain in her hands and the inscription FROM PRISON … TO CITIZENSHIP.[70]

Emmeline felt very optimistic that militancy was over, although the Tax Resistance League, which was set up in 1909 to use the refusal to pay tax as a lobbying tool, continued to take direct action. For example, Miss Clemence Housman, the sister of the activist, writer and artist Laurence Housman, spent several weeks in Holloway for withholding the sum of 4s 6d. Meanwhile, in her brief appeal at the Royal Albert Hall in June 1911, Emmeline managed to raise £100,000, an extremely large fortune in those days.

Much of the action of the suffragette campaign had been carried out on the stage of the Palace of Westminster itself and its immediate environs and the Parliamentary Archives, based in the building, keep a careful record of such activity.

In the summer of 1911 the government no longer attacked the principle of women's suffrage; instead it took a more subtle, nuanced approach. The prime minister Herbert Asquith now took a more positive view in public. However, the Manhood Suffrage Bill, designed to extend votes to working-class men, and not to women of any class, was seen as a direct slap in the face to women's suffrage organisations. Emmeline wrote to Asquith on behalf of the WSPU, proposing a deputation to himself and the Chancellor of the Exchequer David Lloyd George to call for the abandonment of the Manhood Suffrage Bill. In view of the ever-growing pressure of public opinion the deputation, led by Christabel and Emmeline Pankhurst, was received and listened to, but it led to no positive outcome. 'Victimised by such trickery', Emmeline organised yet another mass meeting in the Royal Albert Hall, and yet another deputation of protest by hundreds of women to the House of Commons, where there were 223 arrests. It took several days to dispose of all the cases at Bow Street Police Court, even with the loan of the police billiards room as a waiting room for women on trial. When 200 women finally found their way to Holloway Prison, they seemed no closer to getting the vote.

In the Coronation procession, this banner celebrated those who were prepared to go to prison to win the vote.

However, prison conditions were certainly transformed: Rule243A now gave them something of the status of political prisoners – wearing their own clothes, exercising in freedom, getting themselves up in fancy dress and joking with the wardresses as though they were at a house party. Emmeline found herself arrested before the officer was 'sworn' and, after a week in jail, she was released on bail. On her release she wrote in the paper

> We of the WSPU have dared to affirm the human and divine equality of man and woman. On that affirmation we are prepared to stake our honour, our liberty and our life. Upon that affirmation, we take our stand against all material and spiritual forces of negation and denial.[71]

The temper of the WSPU was now at an all-time high, with letters of encouragement pouring into the office. In December 1911 suffragettes succeeded in completely silencing the prime minister when he was trying to give a speech at the City Temple, stopping him in mid-sentence. 1912 began with the suffrage situation in turmoil, summed up by the *Observer* as 'Splits and Cross Splits'. Each group in the cabinet proclaimed a different point of view on the suffrage. The suffragettes failed to get an answer from Lloyd George or Asquith on the call for a referendum on the suffrage. They were then accused by the anti-suffragist C E H Hobhouse[72] of being less militant than the men who had burnt down Nottingham Castle in opposition to the Reform Act of 1832, or those of the Reform League who had torn down Hyde Park's railings in 1867.

This was like a match to dry tinder. Most passive resistance was now at an end. The first manifestation of militancy was an outbreak of smashing of plate glass windows, with the distinctive sounds of hammering, crashing and splintering. Meanwhile Mrs Pankhurst, and others, carried out a raid with stones to break the windows of government buildings in Downing Street. In connection with this protest more than 200 women were arrested, including the composer Ethel Smyth, who donated her famous 'March of the Women' to the WSPU. As a by-product Fred and Emmeline were arrested in March 1912 during a raid at their flat in Clement's Inn (from which Christabel Pankhurst managed to escape) and taken to Bow Street. Fred's last words to Emmeline before they were parted were 'This is their hour and the power of darkness!'[73] They were charged with conspiring to commit

Fred and Emmeline on their way to the Old Bailey for the Conspiracy Trial in 1911.

*Fred and Emmeline Pethick-Lawrence, Emmeline Pankhurst and Mabel Tuke
in the dock at the Old Bailey for the conspiracy trial in 1912.*

damage and kept in different prisons, Emmeline at Holloway and Fred
at Brixton, for three to four weeks. Emmeline enormously valued the
help and support of the Unitarian Minister Mr Hankinson, who kept
lines of communication open between herself and Fred. When they
returned to court they were released on bail in time for another mass
meeting in the Royal Albert Hall.

Before they went up for trial at the Old Bailey, Emmeline received a
letter from Fred:

> Beloved.
> We are very near to a great day. The greatest we have
> seen in our lives. To me it seems that an honour such as is
> conferred only on a few in many centuries is about to be
> conferred on us. We are to stand where the great and
> noble have stood before us all down the ages. We are to be
> linked with those who have won the everlasting homage
> of the whole human race…
> It is the supreme joy that you and I will stand there
> together, It is the complete and perfect expression of that

faith to which we by our travail are giving birth. It is good that we shall have by our side that great woman who is our friend, who of all women in the world we would wish to have with us in that hour.[74]

This assessment of Mrs Pankhurst is deeply ironic in view of what was about to happen. Christabel meanwhile had gone missing and was being searched for high and low, assuming the status of a fugitive saint.

The Conspiracy Trial opened on 15 May 1912 at the Old Bailey. The defendants were charged on 54 counts, mostly centred on an alleged conspiracy to damage the property of subjects of the King, with Christabel Pankhurst and others accused of damaging the property of the Crown. Fred and Emmeline pleaded not guilty. Fred outlined the case for the defence. It was the Cabinet that was guilty of conspiracy and incitement to conspiracy, not the WSPU, he claimed. He dealt with the history of women's suffrage agitation over the past forty years, and of militant agitation over the last six years. He pointed out that although as a man he could not take part in the agitation, as the WSPU was a women-only organisation, he and other men who stood by to give what help they could 'were saving the movement from becoming a sex war'.

Dr Ethel Smyth was brought out of prison especially to speak on the constitution of the WSPU as a defence witness, and Mrs Pankhurst spoke very movingly about her experience in the movement and the appalling abuses to which women within it had been subjected. All those who heard it, including the jurors, were spell-bound.

Emmeline and Fred were subjected to the ransacking of their private apartment by the police and the seizure of their bank account. The counsel for the defence, T M Healy KC, declared, 'This is a Great State Trial. It is not the women who are on trial. It is the system of Government that is on trial'.[75] In spite of this the defendants were found guilty, and sentenced to nine months in the Second Division. In spite of Emmeline's impassioned plea for clemency, she and Mrs Pankhurst were carried off to jail 'with the heart of thousands of people with us'.[76]

There was widespread indignation at the sentences passed on the Pethick-Lawrences, both in Britain and throughout the world, and outrage that these three 'devoted persons'[77] (Emmeline, Fred and Mrs Pankhurst) should be imprisoned in felons' cells like common criminals. Leaders of the WSPU, including the Pethick-Lawrences, were subsequently moved to the First Division in prison, but the rank and file were retained in the Second Division. It was decided to resume hunger strikes in protest, but prison staff were reluctant to carry out forcible feeding. Only Fred was forcibly fed (in Brixton) and all three of the convicted – first Mrs Pankhurst, then Emmeline, and then Fred – were eventually released. Before their release, Emmeline wrote to Fred from Holloway in almost ecstatic terms, 'with faith in the universal Life of which we partake':

> My surroundings lend colour to the convent idea! My room on the ground floor is vaulted above and partitioned by an arch. There are windows that open top and bottom – in aspect quite ecclesiastical. They look out upon a bank of shrubs and an overshadowing tree, through the leaves of which the morning sunlight shimmers and throws flickering shadows and lights on floor and wall. Behind them is a sunny path and a tiny garden. It is a little shut in, a little dark except on very bright days.
>
> But I feel close to 'Mother Earth' and rejoice once more in that sense of union, so vital to the life of my senses. I hear the blackbirds and thrushes morning and night and can watch a very bold and fat robin lording it over the sparrows. At night I can hear rain falling and trickling through the ground and I can see the brightening sky at dawn, And my earth hunger is appeased.[78]

During a debate in parliament after the Conspiracy Trial Labour backbencher George Lansbury told Asquith that 'You will go down in history as the man who tortured innocent women'.[79]

It was at this point, when the Pethick-Lawrences' position in the WSPU was at its height, that things began to sensationally fall apart.

4. Things Fall Apart

The reasons behind the rift between the Pankhursts and the Pethick-Lawrences in 1912 have been the cause of endless speculation, with almost as many views on the subject as there are people expressing them. What is clear is that it came as a great shock to Fred and Emmeline, and that the whole process was extremely hard on them. Although they had certainly not agreed on every point with the Pankhursts up till then, particularly on the appropriate level of violence to be used during the struggle for women's suffrage, they had not disagreed publicly and had presented a very united front to the world for six years. The Pethick-Lawrences believed that violence against the government was far more effective – and popular – than violence directed against individuals.

Before the dispute broke, Fred and Emmeline were feeling that they must build on the propaganda value of the State Trial 'and organise a great campaign of popular demonstrations which should outdo anything achieved before'. There was overwhelming public demand for this. 'The people were eager to see us and to hear us and to support us.'[1] It was thus a bombshell to discover that the Pankhursts had a completely different vision for the WSPU. Fred and Emmeline were summoned in July 1912 (on their way to recuperate in Switzerland from their prison stays) to meet the Pankhursts in Boulogne (Christabel was already in France, since she had fled to Paris to avoid arrest in March). As they all walked along the cliffs between Boulogne and Wimereux, Mrs Pankhurst announced a new kind of campaign: a widespread attack on public and private property, secretly carried out by suffragettes who would not offer themselves for arrest and who would, wherever possible, make good their escape.

> As our minds had been moving in quite another direction, this project came as a shock to us both, We considered it sheer madness to throw away the immense publicity and propaganda value that the demonstration followed by the State Trial had brought to our cause.[2]

At the same time Helen Craggs (who in 1957 was to become Fred

Pethick-Lawrence's second wife) was arrested for attempting acts of arson against the homes of Cabinet members, apparently on her own initiative.[3]

Fred and Emmeline envisaged the return of Christabel from Paris as a huge propaganda tool against the government. But to the Pethick-Lawrences' dismay Christabel chose to obey her mother's instructions, and stay in Paris to direct the movement from there. This was almost too much for the Pethick-Lawrences, who had had a warm and affectionate relationship with Christabel and regarded her almost as a daughter, as she had stayed in their flat for six years:

> Nerves frayed by the recent ordeal, we found ourselves for the first time in something that resembled a family quarrel... However, we quickly made it up again and parted good friends, agreeing to postpone all discussion of the future until we were in normal health again. But though I did not realize it at the time, a cleavage of the ground had taken place and had left the Pankhursts on one side of the chasm and ourselves on the other. The reason I did not see it then was that I did not dare to look. It meant as I instinctively knew – goodbye to my passionate dream.[4]

Fred and Emmeline had worked with Mrs Pankhurst for six years 'at one with [her] in her objective of women's political emancipation', but in retrospect they recognised there had been cracks in the relationship. In her addiction to militancy, Mrs Pankhurst 'demonstrated that excitement, drama and danger were the conditions in which her temperament found full scope'.[5] For Emmeline, Mrs Pankhurst's idea of 'civil war' was repellent.

Things now moved very quickly, with blow after blow descending relentlessly on the Pethick-Lawrences. Mrs Pankhurst persuaded Fred and Emmeline to go and stay with her brother in Vancouver Island in Canada for a couple of months to keep them out of public life. This trip included a well-received speech by Emmeline at the Colorado State Legislature in Denver, during their homeward journey eastwards across North America. But while they were still in Canada they had discovered that bailiffs were in their house in Surrey to collect money to pay for the legal costs of the conspiracy trial and Mrs Pankhurst wrote to try and persuade them to stay on in Canada and remove all their financial assets from England – an offer Fred and Emmeline unsurprisingly declined.

When they returned to London in October to take part in another Royal Albert Hall event, they were met by a grim-faced friend, who told them that they had been turned out of the WSPU. 'I don't believe it! Impossible! Incredible! You are dreaming!' was Emmeline's appalled response. When she saw Mrs Pankhurst the next day, she was stunned to find all connection between them had been severed. Her previous friends and colleagues, Annie Kenney and Mabel Tuke, also refused to speak to her.

Fred and Emmeline at first pinned their hopes on Christabel, who had lived with them in 'closest intimacy' at Clement's Inn, but Christabel now showed herself to be in complete agreement with her mother. As Christabel herself later explained:

> On the return from Canada of Mr. and Mrs. Pethick-Lawrence there was a consultation in France where I was now definitely established. The outcome of this and a further meeting was the serious announcement that they and we had parted company owing to a difference of opinion as to the policy to be pursued in future by the WSPU. Ownership and control of the paper Votes for Women they retained but their connection with the WSPU organization ceased. This separation on a matter of policy was a cause of deep regret to all concerned.[6]

Christabel told Fred and Emmeline that they could speak at the Royal Albert Hall event but that no other leader, including Mrs Pankhurst, would be present. They could continue to edit *Votes for Women*, but it would no longer be the official voice of the WSPU. Christabel's brief account of this momentous set of events, in her posthumous biography,[7] shows a remarkable lack of understanding or sympathy towards people who had been like parents to her, and who had devoted themselves heart and soul to the WSPU and Votes for Women. Later on, however, she was to try to re-establish a relationship with Emmeline, and they corresponded briefly in the 1920s, when Christabel wrote to Emmeline, rather disingenuously:

> There is no inward change in the love which once united us in the service of the same ideal, the same cause ... Profoundly the love ensures and the value each sets upon what has been seen in the mind and heart of the other.[7]

Prior to 1912, Christabel's relationships with Emmeline and Fred

MR. AND MRS. PETHICK LAWRENCE AND MISS CHRISTABEL
PANKHURST GOING TO BOW STREET, OCTOBER 14, 1908.

The National Women's Social and Political Union,
4, Clements Inn, W.C.

*In the early days Christabel Pankhurst was very close to the Pethick-Lawrences,
who looked on her as a daughter. She stayed in their flat for six years. Another
Pankhurst daughter, Adela, worked closely for a time with Emmeline before
leaving England for Australia in 1914.*

The two Emmelines in happier days – it is hard to believe how they came to fall out with each other so dramatically. The split between Mrs Pankhurst and Emmeline could have been a huge disruption, but Emmeline remained committed to the cause.

within the WSPU had been entirely warm and complimentary. Fred and Emmeline's response to this crisis was astonishing in its lack of rancour. The potential for them to cause harm to the WSPU, and to the whole movement, was enormous. But Fred – with Emmeline in support – chose another path. 'We can no longer be creative in the movement, although we can be destructive. If we appeal to the Union we shall split the ranks. Is it worthwhile?' Emmeline asked rhetorically.[9] They withdrew from the Royal Albert Hall event, but they agreed to continue editing *Votes for Women*.

Another, final, consultation was held in Boulogne between the Pankhursts and the Pethick-Lawrences, which produced a statement, sent to the full committee of the WSPU for approval, which would reduce the damage to the women's movement to a minimum. The statement read:

GRAVE STATEMENT BY THE LEADERS

At the first re-union of the leaders after the enforced holiday, Mrs Pankhurst and Miss Christabel Pankhurst outlined a new militant policy which Mr and Mrs Pethick-Lawrence found themselves altogether unable to approve.

Mrs Pankhurst and Miss Christabel Pankhurst indi-
cated that they were not prepared to modify their inten-
tions and recommended that Mr and Mrs
Pethick-Lawrence resume control of the paper Votes for
Women and should leave the Women's Social and
Political Union...

Rather than make schism in the ranks of the Union Mr
and Mrs Pethick-Lawrence consented to take this
course.[10]

But a letter from Mrs Pankhurst to Emmeline from Boulogne
paints a more complex picture:

It is quite evident that the authorities and also the
Insurance Companies mean to take full advantage of the
fact that they can attack Mr Lawrence with profit, and
through Mr Lawrence weaken the Movement. So long as
Mr Lawrence can be connected with militant acts involving damage to property they will make him pay. Nothing
but the cessation of militancy (which of course is
unthinkable before the vote is assured, or his complete
ruin), will stop this action on their part. They see in Mr
Lawrence a potent weapon against the militant movement
and they mean to use it. This weapon is a powerful one.
By its use they can not only ruin Mr Lawrence, but they
also intend, if they can, to divert our funds. If suffragists,
feeling strongly as they do, the injustice of one having to
suffer for the acts of others, raised a fund to recoup Mr
Lawrence, it would mean that our members' money
would go finally into the coffers of the enemy and the
fighting fund would be depleted or ended. It would also
reduce militancy to a farce for the damage we did with
one hand would be repaired with the other. It is well to
see things at their very worst especially when the very
worst is not only possible but highly likely. In one night,
by one militant act, hundreds of thousands of pounds
might be involved and the only individuals in the
Movement who would be affected apart from imprisonment of those responsible would be you two. So long as
you are a responsible official of this Union this will be
so.[11]

This makes it clear the decision to eject the Pethick-Lawrences was taken by the Pankhursts unilaterally, and was not primarily to do with a disagreement over militancy, as in the official statement. There was no expression of regret, and no message of appreciation for the huge contributions, and sacrifices, that the Pethick-Lawrences had made to the WSPU.

Mrs Pankhurst managed to take command of the meeting at the Royal Albert Hall, prepared to fight on alone without the Pethick-Lawrences, and announced a new policy of destruction of property. It is hard to understand her ruthless treatment of two people who had been so pivotal to the development of the WSPU. Fred had been its business manager, effectively bankrolling the organisation, and had bailed out many arrested suffragettes. Emmeline had been the WSPU's treasurer, fundraiser, creative director and organiser, and a frequent speaker, leader of delegations, and inmate of Holloway Prison. Both of them had served as editors of *Votes for Women* since 1907. As Sylvia Pankhurst wrote:

> Emmeline Lawrence, with her remarkable capacity as a treasurer... 'our treasurer,' Christabel once declared, 'excites the envy of the entire political world'. The income... of the WSPU 'rose with increasing momentum from £3,000 in 1906-7 to more than £25,000 in 1911-12'.[12]

Emmeline tried to analyse Mrs Pankhurst's motivation over this sorry incident in her autobiography. Mrs Pankhurst seemed to be more interested in militancy for its own sake than in the governance of the movement, and how it was organised. Mrs Pankhurst was distressed by the way that Christabel consulted the Pethick-Lawrences about every-thing. She had arrived at the conclusion that the time had come for more revolutionary tactics, and she convinced her daughter to share this view. She concluded that while Fred's money had been a big asset to the WSPU, once the government brought the 'heavy guns' to attack Fred's financial position, which would affect the WSPU financially rather than just him personally, 'it [Fred's wealth] would cease to be a source of strength and would become a source of weakness ... From this Mrs Pankhurst concluded that we should be expelled from the WSPU and go to live in Canada.'[13]

Mrs Pankhurst was fundamentally wrong in thinking more militant action against individuals would strengthen the movement (in fact it brought great hostility in the next two years); whereas previous tactics of attacking Government property (as encouraged by the Pethick-

Lawrences) were very popular. Emmeline summed up Mrs Pankhurst in a very clear-headed way.

> There was something quite ruthless about Mrs Pankhurst and Christabel where human relations were concerned. The ruthlessness was shown not only to us but to many others notably to Sylvia who had given up her career and, without any material compensation whatever, had sacrificed her life to the cause. Men and women of destiny are like that. They are like some force in nature – a tidal wave or a river in full flood. Looking back on these events that happened so long ago, it seems to me a miracle that for six years there could have existed a fourfold partnership like ours in which each member paid a unique and important part.[14]

Although at the time Fred was, like Emmeline, privately very angry and upset over their split with the Pankhursts, and their expulsion from the WSPU, in public he remained unerringly supportive of the Pankhursts for the rest of his life. Thus he was present when Emmeline Pankhurst's statue was inaugurated in Victoria Tower Gardens in 1930, and he even gave a speech at the event. When Christabel Pankhurst's memoir of the militant women's movement was discovered after her death in 1958, Fred took it upon himself to edit the manuscript and he guided it to publication with exceptional generosity, even though he was already in his late eighties. He gave it the title *Unshackled: The Story of How we Won the Vote*, and wrote an extremely generous preface, which was entirely celebratory of Christabel.

In 2018 an image of Fred was one of only four male 'friends of the suffrage' to be represented on the plinth below Gillian Waring's statue of Millicent Fawcett in Parliament Square: the first ever statue in the Square to depict a woman.[15] This acknowledged the key role he had played in the struggle.

As Emmeline reflected:

> Thus in October, 1912, my direct participation in the militant movement came to an end. The cleavage was final and complete. From that time I never saw or heard from Mrs Pankhurst again, and Christabel, who had shared our family life, became a complete stranger. The Pankhursts did nothing by halves.[16]

But there was one member of the Pankhurst family with whom Fred and Emmeline remained closely in touch: Sylvia, Emmeline Pankhurst's other daughter. Sylvia had also fallen out with Mrs Pankhurst after Sylvia had turned the branch of the WSPU in the East End (where Sylvia lived) into an organisation which fought for gender equality on many fronts, rather than just suffrage, including the plight of working-class women and men, and embracing pacifism. Later, in 1927, Sylvia further alienated her mother by giving birth to a child (Richard) outside marriage. The child's father was Silvio Corio, who had lived with Sylvia for years, and Emmeline Pethick-Lawrence paid for Sylvia's stay in the nursing home when she gave birth.

It is a testament to Sylvia's commitment that when asked to choose between her family and her 'mates' in the East End, she chose the latter.[17] The East End branch of the WSPU developed into the East London Federation of the Suffragettes which, as the First World War started to rage, 'was openly socialist, pacifist and internationalist. It empowered hundreds of people and inspired thousands more … it was a true mass movement for women's rights and equality.'[18] The federation encompassed and fought for housing – most East End housing being atrocious and in very poor repair, employment (most women's work being grossly underpaid and often dangerous), and nurseries for children. It set up a factory for making toys, a cut-price restaurant, and once the First World War had started, it marched and gathered against conscription, and for the vote. The whole enterprise was kept together by a newspaper which Sylvia edited from January 1914, after the East London Suffragettes split with the WSPU. The newspaper started life as the *Women's Dreadnought*:

> The name of our paper, The Women's Dreadnought, is symbolic of the fact that the women who are fighting for freedom must fear nothing… The chief duty of the Dreadnought will be to deal with the franchise question from the working women's point of view…[19]

The paper was published weekly, and in 1917 it changed its name to the *Workers' Dreadnought*, and widened its scope.

> [O]ver its decade-long existence its focus expanded to include national and international politics, war, peace and revolution. In its first few months 20,000 copies were printed each week, but the circulation was reduced to 10,000 after the outbreak of war when the cost of paper

An anti-suffrage comic card depicts a suffragette wearing a green hat, purple coat and white spats, wielding a hammer and smashing a department store window. The movement became increasingly militant and violent, with arson attacks, and attacks on works of art (such as the Rokeby Venus).

rose sharply… As well as providing a channel for the Federation to reach current and potential members in the East End with their campaign messages, the paper quickly took on an important role as a platform for the voices of working women and men to be heard and as a way to draw attention to injustices.[20]

Remarkably the Pethick-Lawrences remained loyal to the movement, and outwardly loyal to all the Pankhursts for the rest of their lives, never speaking publicly against them. Emmeline's letter sent on 17 October 1912 is also far from angry:

> Those who know me and my husband will understand that our thought in taking the action that we have is for the good and welfare of the Movement to which we dedicated all that we had of life or fortune six years ago. We leave it for the same reason that we entered it – to serve it without regard to our own interests.[21]

But if Fred and Emmeline's direct participation in the fight for women's suffrage was over from 1912 onwards, they both remained keenly interested in the movement. They certainly remained in the news. For example, a 1912 *Punch* cartoon depicted two earnest ladies in a tea room: One asks the other, 'Are you a Peth or a Pank?' and for a time this question became common currency among the gossiping classes. Most press coverage was hostile.

But the shock of the severance was very hard. It was the shock of the loss of colleagues and friends, and of the organisation itself which as 'our special creation Fred and I [had] loved as though it were our child'.[22] Some of the pain of loss was assuaged by their continued editorship of *Votes for Women* to which they remained devoted, even after the WSPU brought out *The Suffragette* (in 1912) as the official opposition (circulation was 17,000 for the first edition, falling to 7,500 following the first pillar box incidents, which involved the destruction of letters in post boxes by chemicals in Fleet Street). They then became enmeshed in the drama over the Conspiracy Trial, and the attempt to reclaim money from Fred. The Pethick-Lawrences only found out, while recuperating from prison in Canada, that the government had sent bailiffs to The Mascot, their country house at Holmwood in Surrey. Although Fred knew that it would have been much easier, and less costly, to write a cheque in payment of the whole amount, he came to the conclusion that to submit to these arbitrary and unjust proceedings would be contrary to the spirit of the militant movement.

An auction was arranged for 31 October 1912, and Holmwood's furniture was sold for a sum of £300. 'Members of my family and a few personal friends bought most of the furniture and articles of particular associations and value, and returned them to us as a gift', Emmeline later recalled,[23] and the auctioneer himself was inspired to return one article he had bought as a keepsake. The *Financial News* pointed out the injustice of a citizen being held financially responsible for a prosecution, while the Public Prosecutor is wholly immune and not liable for costs if a prosecution fails.

Fred was then hammered by one financial blow after another – a civil action to recover the balance of the claim, the seizing of his accounts, and a petition in bankruptcy. He refused to pay this unjust penalty, because he felt that the actions of the Government were politically motivated, with the sole aim of crushing their opponents. Fred became a financial cipher, until such time as the amount of his fine was deducted from his property and he became discharged from bankruptcy. In the meantime Fred and Emmeline were taken to court for damaging windows in March 1913, and were allowed to defend themselves. The judge, Mr Justice Darling, referred to Emmeline's speech as 'a most eloquent speech, really one of the most eloquent I have ever heard', and in his summing up he concluded, 'These women are just as

An anti-suffragette postcard tried to turn the campaign into a joke, in an attempt to make them seem ridiculous

much entitled to ask for the vote as the men are'.[24]

In spite of a sympathetic judge Fred was found guilty, and payments were taken for the full amount of the prosecution costs. His bankruptcy was accordingly annulled, although his compulsory resignation from membership of the Reform Club was not restored, and he eventually had to seek another club.

Emmeline reflected on what this had all cost him:

> Thus he underwent every variation of the sacrifice demanded for the freedom of women – imprisonment – hunger strike – forcible feeding – bankruptcy – loss of financial substance – expulsion from his club. All this he went through unflinchingly on account of the faith that was in him. I have always been glad that deep as is the love between us he never took up the women's cause for my sake but as a result of our common outlook. His reward has been the appreciation and friendship, in the emancipation of women.[25]

With hindsight, it is amusing to read that 'expulsion from his club' is listed alongside 'imprisonment', 'forcible feeding' and 'loss of financial substance' in this litany of indignities: Fred's membership of a gentleman's club was clearly very important to him, even as a Labour man.

In 1913, news of the breach between the Pankhursts and the Pethick-Lawrences, became public although the press showed remarkable restraint and, 'owing to the policy of silence loyally carried out on both sides, gossip quickly died down.'[26] Meanwhile the militant movement gained momentum, with new methods of violent protest including the destruction of letters in post boxes by chemicals, and the spectacular bombing and burning of haystacks, churches and places of historic and public interest, such as Lloyd George's unfinished house in Surrey, the railway station at Oxted in Surrey, and the empty Church of St Catherine's in Hatcham, south London.

In January 1913 the government's Franchise Reform Bill (a small step forwards the franchise) was due to be presented to Parliament but had to be withdrawn. Due to a universal outcry, Herbert Asquith, going back on all he had publicly said to the contrary, suggested alternatives like a Private Members' or a new Conciliation Bill. These were considered as valueless by every section of the suffrage movement. After a huge public meeting by the non-militant suffragists in the Queen's Hall, some took part again in violent action: a prominent Liberal woman Mrs Cobden Hirst broke the windows of the Home

PROOF.

The Director of Public Prosecutions v. F. W. Pethick Lawrence.

"The Mascot,"

HOLMWOOD, SURREY

NEAR DORKING.

CATALOGUE

OF

THE CONTENTS

OF THE ABOVE

Well=furnished Residence

IN EARLY ENGLISH STYLE

INCLUDING

Oak and Enamelled Bedroom Suites

And Bedsteads,

DRAWING AND DINING ROOM FURNITURE

Chesterfield Settee, Lounge and Easy Chairs.

Full Compass Piano by Bechstein

Small Library of Books, Pictures and Ornaments,
Wines and Spirits

A QUANTITY OF A.1. PLATE

Linen, China and Glass, Copper Culinary Utensils, and numerous
other effects.

G. M. FRIEAKE

WILL SELL BY AUCTION AS ABOVE, ON

Thursday, October 31st, 1912,

At ONE o'clock precisely.

May be viewed day prior and Morning of Sale.   Catalogues may be had at

89, Chancery Lane, W.C.

WILSONS, Printers, Gray's Inn Passage, Red Lion Street, Holborn, W.C.

The notice of sale of Fred and Emmeline's belongings in their house The Mascot on October 31 1912. Well-wishers bought the items auctioned to return to the Pethick-Lawrences.

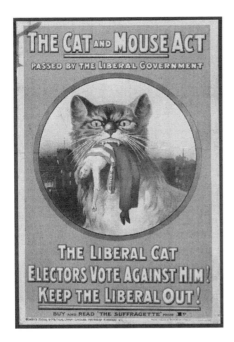

The government was accused of playing cat and mouse to the campaigners: the intention of the hated "Cat and Mouse" Act was to reduce the need for forced feeding, stories about which generated increasing public support for the suffrage campaign. Those women who went on hunger strike were temporarily released, and when restored to health were rearrested to resume their prison sentence. The Act was extremely unpopular.

Office. One woman cited the fact that parliament had voted an income of £400 a year for MPs, and that this salary was paid by women taxpayers as well as men.

Meanwhile, opinion was rising against forcible feeding, and in response the Government brought in the Prisoners' Temporary Discharge Bill – commonly known as the 'Cat and Mouse Bill' – which gave the authorities power to release those whose health was in danger when they went on hunger strike; under the terms of the bill, they could then be re-arrested later, after they had recovered. This may have removed the need for forcible feeding, but it was intensely unpopular, and was roundly condemned in an editorial in *Votes for Women*. George Bernard Shaw, an ardent supporter of the newspaper, delivered an impassioned speech against the Cat and Mouse Bill:

> I have always believed in the old simple statement that we
> are all members one of another. If you take a woman and
> torture her you torture me ... I tell you that these denials
> of fundamental rights are really a violation of the soul.[27]

An independent committee, which included Emmeline, was put together to fight the Cat and Mouse Bill and a deputation (including Emmeline and Evelyn Sharp of *Votes for Women*) assembled to go to the House of Commons with a memorial to the Home Secretary, Reginald

McKenna, and a request for an interview with him. When this was refused Emmeline organised an open-air protest outside the Strangers' Entrance and was arrested, charged and sentenced to a fortnight's imprisonment. This was subsequently reduced to two days, partly because of the involvement of Lady Sybil Smith, a society lady who was sympathetic to the cause, dedicated to non-violence, and had friends in high places. As Emmeline put it, 'thus ended my sixth and last imprisonment in Holloway Jail.'[28] She and Evelyn Sharp were happy that this occasion had been used to follow up *Votes for Women*'s editorial protest against the Cat and Mouse Act by action.

The Home Secretary Reginald McKenna had to face a torrent of criticism on the Cat and Mouse Act. All attempts to supress the WSPU failed, but in June 2013 the death of Emily Wilding Davison under the King's horse at the Derby, and her subsequent funeral, struck the movement into an awed silence. The occasion was marked by a massive procession of mourners, wearing, not black, but the suffragette colours of purple, white and green in recognition of the cause for which Emily had died. The funeral received national coverage.[29]

Meanwhile, the newspaper *Votes for Women* was widening its scope to include the situation in Ireland, where the struggle for independence was then at its height, and the plight of those suffering extreme poverty, such as the widow who confined her four children to an underground room out of poverty rather than neglect. *Votes for Women* took the case of the impoverished widow up not only so that an individual wrong might be righted, but also to highlight the need for a national pension to allow widows to bring up their children decently, a cause Emmeline advocated for much of her life.

In the autumn of 1913 six little girls, rendered destitute by the outbreak of severe Labour troubles in Dublin, were brought by Emmeline to stay for three months at The Sundial, the holiday house for women and children which Fred and Emmeline had built in the grounds of The Mascot, their Surrey home. Emmeline kitted them out in little green outfits, and they stayed until things improved at home. When Emmeline came to speak about suffrage in Dublin in January 1914, the girls turned out at the meeting, wearing their green outfits, to greet her.[30]

In early 1914 a great many events took place on the suffrage front, including a deputation to Asquith on the Cat and Mouse Act. When the Prime Minister refused to speak to the deputation, they gathered in Parliament Square where the speakers, including Laurence Housman, who was always ready to speak in public, Lord Rhondda (a Welsh Industrialist and Liberal politician) and the war correspondent Henry

The funeral of Emily Wilding Davison saw a great outpouring of grief.
[Museum of London]

Nevinson – were each in turn taken into custody. In June 1914 a new suffrage society – the United Suffragists – was formed: many prominent men and women joined the society, many of whom had not previously identified with the suffrage movement. In June the manifesto of the United Suffragists came out, with 31 distinguished vice-Presidents, including Emmeline Pethick-Lawrence, and in July there was a great meeting in Kingsway Hall in London, where in a speech Emmeline declared that she and Fred had joined the United Suffragists, and were bringing *Votes for Women* with them.

Fred and Emmeline were now planning a worldwide tour to learn at first hand the conditions affecting women in the United States, Canada, Australia, New Zealand, China and Japan. Meanwhile Sylvia Pankhurst managed after multiple hunger strikes to get herself close to an audience with Asquith, who began to show some willingness to speak to her delegation about suffrage, declaring he was in complete agreement with them on their demand for a democratic suffrage measure.

Then, in the midst of this more hopeful scenario, another more dramatic, catastrophe struck in the summer of 1914: the First World War.

5. Peace campaigner. 'Pow-Wows With The Fraus'

On 4 August, 'war was declared and the world in which we lived and dreamed and worked was shattered to bits… Divisions and conflicts were forgotten while the whole nation was united in the one purpose of serving our county in her hour of danger.'[1] The effect of the declaration of war on the suffragette movement was dramatic. Mrs Pankhurst declared that 'The Union would suspend activities… Money and energy would thus be saved,' and an opportunity was to be taken to 'recuperate after the tremendous strain and suffering of the past two years.'[2] Emmeline and Christabel Pankhurst, and a loyal following of suffragettes, devoted themselves enthusiastically to war work, including the issue of enlistment, the recruitment of men into the armed forces, and the employment of women in munitions factories. The WSPU was wound up in 1917 with its remaining funds going into an adoption home for female children. This truce in militancy surprised many, but Emmeline and Christabel Pankhurst were, essentially, deeply conservative in their political views, and 'gung-ho' in their attitude to a nation at war.

It is tempting to define the Pethick-Lawrences' relationship to the militant suffragette movement by their traumatic ejection from the WSPU, but this should never undermine the fact that their involvement in the Suffragette Movement had been unequivocal and crucial since 1906, when Mrs Pankhurst came down from Manchester to establish the WSPU in London. While Emmeline Pethick-Lawrence led the way, Fred followed and their devotion to, and involvement. in the WSPU was total. They had allowed their flat in Clement's Inn to be used as the WSPU's headquarters – with an increasing number of rooms being taken to accommodate the organisation's growth – as well as providing a home for Christabel Pankhurst, fundraising for the movement and defending individual suffragettes.

One of the side effects of the war in Britain was that it divided the women's movement. While Mrs Pankhurst and many of her supporters in the WSPU abandoned the cause of women's suffrage to throw themselves into enthusiastic support for the war effort, others were equally convinced that the war was more likely to end civilisation than to save it. Emmeline Pethick-Lawrence's first response to the outbreak of war (which she described as 'one of the most vivid experiences I have ever known')[3] was to join the Women's Emergency Corps Committee, founded by suffragette and aid worker Evalina Haverfield and the singer and actress Decima Moore. The aims of the Women's Emergency Corps seemed laudable at first: to assist the war effort by training women doctors, nurses, and motorcycle messengers. But Emmeline soon became convinced not only of the need to contribute to the war effort but also of the need to stand up against the war. This was precipitated by a visit early in the war from the Hungarian suffragist Rosika Schwimmer, who wanted to get to America to persuade women there to take the initiative in pleading for efforts towards negotiation on the part of the neutral countries.

In October 1914 Emmeline was invited to New York City to speak at a large suffrage meeting in Carnegie Hall. She saw this as an opportunity to enlist the support of the suffrage movement in America to lobby for world peace, secured by negotiation. With the support of women like the lawyer Madeleine Doty (with whom Emmeline felt a special affinity) and the prominent peace campaigner Chrystal Eastman, who was involved in setting up the Women's International League of Peace and Freedom (WILPF), this led to the formation of the Women's Peace Party of New York. This in turn drew in Jane Addams, America's most famous peace campaigner, widely recognised as the 'most influential woman in America'. From New York, Emmeline went on to attend the Washington Conference in early 1915, which was organised to constitute a national movement of all the local women's parties that had formed as a result of her meetings in the United States. Here Jane Addams consented (albeit reluctantly, being a woman of great humility) to take on the national presidency of the Women's Peace Party.

Meanwhile Dr Aletta Jacobs, the first woman doctor in Holland and a member of the Women's International Suffrage Alliance, proposed to bring together women from America and Europe (from both belligerent and non-belligerent countries) at a Women's Peace Congress in the Hague. In February 1915 she met up with other internationally-known women from other countries to plan this event (due to be held on 28 April), and draw up resolutions.

Early in April more than 50 representatives from the National Peace Party of America embarked for the Hague on the liner *Noordam* with Jane Addams, Madeleine Doty, Rosika Schwimmer – and Emmeline and Fred (who had been with Emmeline in the US since Christmas). The Mayor of New York presented them with a PEACE flag, which

Emmeline addressing a crowd in Trafalgar Square

was hoisted on the *Noordam* as they left New York harbour. They were stopped in Dover by order of the British Government but the American ambassador intervened, and they were allowed to continue at their own risk to Rotterdam.

When they reached Rotterdam the Pethick-Lawrences were nearly barred from entry because they did not have passports (which had only recently been made compulsory). The impasse was fortunately resolved, and Emmeline was able, with two other British women – the lawyer and suffragist Chrystal Macmillan and suffragist Kathleen Courtney – to attend the Conference. A hundred and fifty other 'notable' women (including Sylvia Pankhurst and Olive Schreiner) were prevented from crossing the channel by the government, on the grounds that shipping lanes were closed, and so never made it to the conference. Macmillan and Courtney only managed to attend because they were already there for the initial conference planning in February.

The response of the newspapers was to treat the Hague Peace Conference as some sort of joke – a 'pow-wow with the fraus' – while Emmeline Pankhurst thundered against 'the-peace-at-any-price crowd...', aghast 'that English women should meet German women to discuss terms of peace while the husbands, sons and brothers of those women ... are murdering our men'.[4] Meanwhile, in east London

*Dr Aletta Jacobs, the first woman
doctor in the Netherlands, and
organiser of the Hague Congress.*

Sylvia Pankhurst was exposing the number of soldiers who were being executed for desertion. The views of Sylvia and Emmeline Pankhurst could now hardly be further apart, both on the matter of peace and the many other questions where they were at different ends of a political spectrum. Sylvia was now a confirmed socialist and follower of the Labour leader Keir Hardie, while Emmeline Pankhurst was quite the reverse: she may have started out as a Liberal, but if anything she now moved further to the right.

The Congress in the Hague opened on April 28 1915 with more than thirteen hundred people present – from Austria, Belgium, Canada, Denmark, Germany, Great Britain, Hungary, Italy, the Netherlands, Norway, Sweden and the US. In spite of reporters expecting 'incidents', everything passed peacefully in an atmosphere of 'sympathetic harmony'.[5] The preamble to the resolutions which came out of the Congress stated:

> This International Congress of Women of different nations, classes, creeds and parties is united in expressing sympathy with the suffering of all, whatever their nationality, who are fighting for their country or labouring under the burden of war. Since the mass of the people in each of the countries now at war believe themselves to be fighting not as aggressors, but in self-defence, there can be

no irreconcilable differences between them; and their common ideas afford a basis upon which an honourable peace might be established. The Congress therefore urges the Governments of the world to put an end to bloodshed and begin peace negotiations.[6]

The first resolution to come out of the Congress read:

We the women of the world, in International Congress assembled, protest against the madness and the horror of war, involving as it does a reckless sacrifice of human life and the destruction of so much that humanity has laboured through centuries to build up.[7]

A later resolution found its way into Article 3 of the constitution of the Women's International League for Peace and Freedom (WILPF), which owed its foundation to the Congress in the Hague. What follows was an absolutely key concept of both the Congress, and the organisation which came out of it:

WILPF sees as its ultimate goal the establishment of an international economic order founded on the principle of meeting the needs of all people and not those of profit and privilege.[8]

The Congress of 28 April took place against the backdrop of the sixth day of the second Battle of Ypres, one of the First World War's most costly and futile engagements, which was then raging 100 miles to the south of the Hague. The battle left 122,000 men dead and wounded and ended in stalemate, which only underlined the urgency of what was being discussed.

Over the three days of the Conference twelve resolutions were discussed under seven headings:

1. Women and war
2. Actions towards peace
3. Principles of permanent peace
4. International co-operation
5. The education of children
6. Women and the Peace Settlement Conference
7. Action to be taken

The German delegation to the International Congress of Women at the Hague in 1915. Mrs Pankhurst was furious about fraternising with the German women.

The Congress provided an analysis of the causes of war. Resolutions (contained in a report of over 300 pages, published in English, French and German) dwelt on the horrors of war and its specific effects on women. Suggested actions focused on international justice and the full participation of women in creating a permanent peace. The principles of such a peace incorporated respect for nationality, arbitration and conciliation, international pressure, democratic control of foreign policy and the enfranchisement of women. This was extremely progressive policy-making, but the women who took part in this conference were desperately afraid that their voices would not be heard in the negotiations over the peace talks and that their post-war needs would not be met. Tragically, they were later proved right.

On the last day of the Congress, envoys were appointed to carry the message of the Congress – that war should be brought to an end, not by exhaustion but by negotiation – to the rulers of both belligerent and neutral countries. Amongst these envoys were Jane Addams and Emily Balch (from America), Dr Aletta Jacobs (from Holland), Dr Anita Augsburg and Lida Heymann (from Germany), Chrystal Macmillan, Kathleen Courtney, and the suffragist and writer Catherine Marshall (from England), and the fashion designer Rose Genoni (from Italy). They travelled around Europe, and met with prime ministers and foreign secretaries who listened to them with courtesy – and occasionally with warmth:

On one occasion, Jane Addams remarked to a harassed

and overburdened statesman 'You must think us mad to intrude upon you like this!' His reply was 'Madame, it is we who are mad. You only are sane'.[9]

But in spite of kind words like these, the opportunity for peace by negotiation was missed, and the envoys went back to work on reconciliation in their own countries. Madeleine Doty managed to establish a strong relationship with peace groups in Germany, and in 1916 she was back in Germany distributing relief funds to starving children. Jane Addams returned to the United States after the Congress, and achieved her greatest success when she was received by US President Woodrow Wilson, who hailed the resolutions she brought from the Hague. He adopted nine of them as part of his famous Fourteen Points that served as the basis of the First World War peace negotiations.[10] But in April 1919, during the peace negotiations he re-read and re-thought the new diplomacy, so her effort was to no avail.

After the Congress Emmeline Pethick-Lawrence went back to England and devoted herself to the development of the Women's International League of Great Britain. This was formed, with the words 'Peace and Freedom' added to the organisation's name, at a conference in Westminster in the autumn of 1915. Emmeline became its honorary treasurer. She wrote that 'from this time forward the main purpose of my life was to spread as far as possible the conviction that peace and negotiation alone could promote a stable condition in Europe.'[11]

The International Congress of Women at the Hague 1915

The League (WILPF) soon established 34 branches across Britain, with two or three thousand members, but approaches to Lloyd George, prime minister from December 1916 onwards, were totally unproductive. Emmeline did better with the troops. She published an anti-war letter in the English magazine *The Nation*, and was approached soon after by a young officer on behalf of his soldiers in the field, who had all read the letter and wished him to convey their thanks to Emmeline for writing it. Emmeline was deeply touched. It was clear that many men on the front in France felt that women had left them to their fate. The officer was returning to the front and would probably not see her again, but he implored her 'in the name of the men fighting in the field – carry on with your campaign at home.' He was killed in action soon afterwards.[12]

In 1918 towards the end of the war, a partial victory on women's sugffrage was won, without the WSPU, which had closed down for the duration. The suffragist leader Millicent Fawcett led a deputation of women's and other organisations to meet Lloyd George, and on 10 January 1918 Fawcett witnessed the debate in the House of Lords which resulted in the passing of the women's suffrage clause of the Representation of the People Bill. This passed through both Houses and became the law of the land on 6 February. It was certainly not everything women had been asking for: the vote was given only to women householders, and unmarried or widowed women, with property. For those without property, only the wives of male local government electors, over the age of 30, were enfranchised. But compared with the total failure of the last fifty or more years (Millicent Fawcett had been campaigning for the suffrage since 1866, years before the birth of the WSPU), it was a massive cause for celebration.

The Representation of the People Act was followed quite rapidly by the Parliamentary Qualification Act of November 1918, which allowed women to be elected as Members of Parliament. The speed of the second act caused surprise to many, but it made sense that the electors could also be elected. The new resolution was, in Millicent Fawcett's opinion, 'the logical result of enfranchising women'.[13] However, the legislation came too late to have much effect on the number of women standing in the December 1918 election (known as the 'khaki' or 'coupon election') – the first general election since 1910 – and most women stood as independents as there was no time to be adopted by the major parties. In the event only one woman, Countess Constance Markiewicz, a republican who took part in the Easter Rising of 1916, was elected for Fianna Fail. She never took her seat.[14]

Christabel Pankhurst stood for parliament in Smethwick in

December 1918 as the Women's Party candidate, but lost narrowly to the Labour candidate. She never stood for parliament again and became a preacher of the Second Coming, mainly in America, having fought moral campaigns on chastity, prostitution and venereal disease. (She had published her controversial book *The Great Scourge and How to End It* on venereal disease in 1913). It is notable that a number of suffragettes adopted extreme or 'off the wall' views in later life.

Emmeline already had had experience of a contentious parliamentary campaign. During the War, in March 1917, Fred (who as a conscientious objector had been working for a local farmer in Surrey) was persuaded to stand on a 'Peace by Negotiation' ticket at a by-election in Aberdeen (Fred's autobiography gives no reasons why he was chosen for this seat, with which he appears to have no connections). This turned out to be a hateful experience:

> It was the longest election contest that I ever experienced and the most difficult and unpleasant. The mind of the overwhelming majority of people had been so poisoned by war propaganda and by 'atrocity', rumours that it was closed to reason. I addressed groups of women, but, speaking generally, women were even more embittered than men, and since the being of women is usually wrapped up in husband, brothers or sons, their indignation was not altogether surprising to me.[15]

In the event, in spite of support from leading Labour leaders (such as Ramsay MacDonald), the election campaign was marked by considerable violence and Fred only secured a few hundred votes on polling day. He and Emmeline retreated to Holmwood, their country house in Surrey, to recuperate.

So Emmeline could have guessed what to expect when the Labour Party invited her to stand as their candidate in the Rusholme division of Manchester in the December 1918 election, only a few weeks after the Armistice. Despite Fred's experience in Scotland, Emmeline bravely agreed to stand but only because 'an opportunity was offered to explain publicly the reasons why I believed that the only chance of permanent peace in Europe lay in a just settlement after the war.'[16] She enlisted her pacifist friend Max Plowman, writer of *A Subaltern on the Somme* (a stark account of life in the trenches), to help run her campaign.

War fever was at its height in Rusholme, with election slogans like 'Hang the Kaiser' and 'Make Germany Pay' displayed on all sides. Emmeline soon learnt a painful principle of democracy: the women she had struggled so hard to enfranchise were overwhelmingly in favour of post-war revenge, and they voted against her in droves:

> It was a strange experience for one who had given eight years of life as I had, in the endeavour to win votes for women, to watch working-class mothers, with their babies and small children, eagerly going to the poll to record their votes against me.[17]

Ironically the group who did give their votes wholeheartedly to Emmeline were the troops who were not yet demobilised, and it was they who ensured she did not lose her deposit. The by-election was won easily by the Conservative candidate Robert Burdon Stoker (who had been endorsed by the coalition government) who gained 65% of the vote, with the Liberal candidate trailing with just 19% and Emmeline on 15%).[18]

Emmeline's assessment of the outcome was stark: 'The electors on that day voted, although they did not know it, for another world war [making] The Treaty of Versailles an instrument of vengeance'.[19]

In April 1919 Emmeline chaired a protest meeting in Trafalgar Square on behalf of WILPF, against the hunger blockades which were causing so much misery in Germany: during the course of the war, the Royal Navy's blockade caused the death by starvation of hundreds of thousands of civilians. She then marched with two others with a resolution to Downing Street accompanied by an escort of sympathetic soldiers.

Since the war had ended Emmeline was able to make good her pledge to meet up with friends and colleagues from the Hague Conference in 1915. This reunion took place at the Second International Congress which took place in Zurich on 12-17 May 1919 (attended by representatives of both belligerent and non-belligerent states, with Germany well represented). The Zurich Conference was deliberately held at the same time as the official Peace Conference in Paris (which led to the Treaty of Versailles), attended by Heads of State and foreign ministers who took it upon themselves to determine the fate of Europe. Compared with the small group of women who made it to Zurich, many thousands of delegates and support staff (few of them women) attended the Conference:

> ...the winners gathered in January 1919 to divide the spoils. The number of negotiators and their entourages of secretaries, cooks, valets, translators, messengers, chauf-

Delegates to the 1919 Zurich Conference: their hope was to mitigate the punitive terms of the Treaty of Versailles.

feurs, and guards soared into thousands – the British Empire's mission alone totalled 524 – for many branches of every Allied government wanted a hand in reshaping the world. The Paris Peace Conference lasted, with a few breaks, for a full year, and out of it came a string of treaties and decisions that helped determine the course of the next 20 years and speed the way to a second, wider, more ruinous war.[20]

The women who gathered in Zurich made attempts to lobby the delegates in Paris. They may have been encouraged by President Wilson who met a delegation of French women, with support from other countries, demanding that women should be involved in negotiations at the Peace Conference, but their hopes were dashed when the president showed no sign of acceding to their demands.[21]

Emmeline declared the Zurich Congress to be the most moving experience of her life, bringing together the evidence of the misery and starvation suffered by so many all over Europe 'with the splendid spirit of friendship, courage and hope'[22] of the women who made it there, although this spirit was somewhat countered by the despairing news coming out of Paris:

I for one, believed then, and believe now, that until the
Nations who dictated the Versailles peace have atoned for
the wrongs they inflicted upon the defeated peoples, a
nemesis will rest upon the world. When I remember the
greed-inspired lie that was given currency in 1918 – the lie
that the whole guilt of the war rested upon one nation
who, for this reason, should be forced to pay the whole
cost of it...[23]

As the war was over, and borders were officially open, it was much
easier to get to Zurich, in the neutral country of Switzerland, than it
had been to get to the Hague in 1915, although there were some post-
war 'disruptions' and many delegates, especially those coming from
devastated areas, found their journeys very difficult and arrived late.
But women, who for the last four years had worked for peace in small
isolated groups in their own countries, often in a very hostile environment, were delighted to have the opportunity to come together again
and draw strength from each other in Zurich. In the event around a
hundred women from all over the world, from as far afield as USA and
Uruguay, made the journey.

The Congress was held in Zurich's renowned Glockenhof Hotel
and chaired by Jane Addams. It was meticulously organised in advance
by Addams, Aletta Jacobs and Chrystal Macmillan, on behalf of the
National Committee of Women for Permanent Peace. Over the five
days it covered a wide range of subjects, with the terms of peace, the
need for a League of Nations, and the need to abandon conscription
being constant themes. Clara Ragaz, a noted Swiss pacifist, gave a welcoming address and was confident that the conference would be conducted 'in a spirit of mutual love and respect', the same spirit as she
wished for the future League of Nations.[24]

The Congress in Zurich included the setting up of a number of
carefully-constituted committees on political relations. Political
Committee A concentrated heavily on the urgent need for a League of
Nations, with its associated Women's Covenant:

We believe that the Congress should use its influence
towards the development of this great new agency for a
peaceful evolution in international relations, so that it
may become a true Society of Nations.[25]

Emmeline played an active part throughout the Congress and in
Political Committee B, which concentrated on the disastrous, punitive

conditions that were to be later imposed on Germany at Versailles, which will 'provoke suffering enough to cause anarchy and ruin for generations').[26] It was to this Committee that Emmeline made her impassioned plea for the second resolution:

RESOLUTION ON THE BLOCKADE AND
FAMINE

This International Congress of women regards the tragic situation of widespread unemployment, famine and pestilence extending throughout great tracts of Central and East Europe and through parts of Asia, as a profound disgrace to civilisation, and a challenge to all men and women who believe in the brotherhood of mankind and in the duties of world citizenship.

This Congress appeals to all the Governments of all the Powers now assembled at the Peace Conference in Paris shall be developed into an international organisation for purposes of peace, and that immediate action shall be taken:

That the blockade be immediately lifted, in order that food and raw materials may be brought to the unemployed and starving peoples.

That all the resources of the world, food, raw materials, finance, transport, shall be organised immediately for the relief of the people from famine and pestilence, just in the same way that all the resources of the allied countries have been organised for the relief of the peoples from "the yoke of militarism", so that in this way a great demonstration be given that nations can co-operate and organise to save life as efficiently as they can co-operate and organise to destroy life.

That the lives of millions of starving children shall be saved, regardless of the financial cost. That, if there is an insufficiency of food or of transport facilities to supply all demands, luxuries shall not be allowed transport from one country to another until the necessities of life are supplied to all: and the people of every country be rationed, in order that all the starving shall be fed.

We believe that immediate international action carried out on this scale would not only do more than anything else to satisfy the conscience of humanity at the present moment, but would do more than anything else to heal the wounds of the world and bring about reconciliation and union of all the peoples.[27]

This resolution was later tightened up and shortened before being sent to Paris – and Emmeline was subsequently appointed to a new Political Committee.

Later in the week, on Thursday May 15, Emmeline presented a resolution to organise a great protest meeting in Zurich, with smaller meetings to be held in individual countries. All resolutions of protest were to be sent to Versailles where the Treaty was due to be signed on 15 June. And in an evening meeting on the Friday she made this passionate claim:

> They tell us sometimes that war will never be eradicated because war is a deep instinct of the human heart. I do not believe it: it is not true … War, which is organised murder, is repulsive to every fully-developed human being.
>
> War is a hypnotism which takes possession of a people and the hatred engendered by war is artificially fostered by every possible means, both through the press and through all possible channels … War could not exist in the world if it were not bolstered up by the forcible suppression of the truth.[28]

On the Friday evening, 16 May, Emmeline was scheduled to speak as part of a panel in St Peter's Church, at a meeting that was rather hopefully entitled 'Woman's Part in the Reconstruction of the World'. She was later involved, with the pacifist and politician Margaret Ashton, in finalising the text of the 'Blockade' Resolution and forwarding it to Versailles, though with little response.

The Zurich Congress ranged widely – not just over opposition to war and conscription, and the need for a League of Nations (which should not be a 'League of Conquerors against the conquered') – but a range of progressive social policies, many of them way ahead of their time.[29] These included a 'living wage', 'protection of maternity' (benefits, leave, shortened hours), and 'protection of childhood and youth' (free education for all up to the age of 15, no child labour by under-15s, and 15-18-year-olds to not be employed at night or in unhealthy industries), 'Unemployment' ('the fight against unemployment shall be systematically undertaken; a system of social insurance shall provide against unemployment however caused'), 'social insurance' against sickness, accident or disability to be compulsory for all workers of both sexes; free medical and associated care; insurance for old age – old age pension benefits for widows, 'trade unions' (the right to form every-where, right to strike guaranteed, shop-stewards and work-councils to be instituted).

One delegate to the Zurich Conference was Annot Robinson – a Scottish socialist, feminist and pacifist, and a member of the WSPU – who had been imprisoned for trying to break into parliament. Her let-ters from Zurich to her sister, Nellie, give a vivid description of what it felt like to be an active participant in the Congress, and are a poignant reminder of the hope so cruelly foiled by the men negotiating the Versailles treaty:

> The German delegation was 23 in number and had some interesting women. The French govt. only permitted two to get through: one Mlle Melis from Arras was an orator. In Zurich there were fears of revolution and while we were there three regiments were drafted into the town.[30]

In another letter, Robinson wrote that she saw a 'young subeditor man' who said that there was great unease in Paris and that disorder was pending.

> The Congress was very inspiring. A delegation is in Paris waiting to lay before the Big Four a resolution for the con-gress protesting against the food blockade and the Peace Terms and asking that a Woman's Charter be inserted in the League of Nations. Jane Addams is really very fine, a very quiet motherly-looking woman with great patience and kindness – she needed these qualities to deal with the language difficulties.
>
> There was no evidence of ill-will between the nations, only a most evident effort to understand each other's point of view. The German and Austrian women were evidently suffering from privation and some of the details given by Red Cross Swiss women of conditions in Austria and Romania were appalling. I was much impressed by the Scandinavian women – they were so capable. There was a tendency to relapse into English and indeed the Congress was carried through mainly in English and German. I was chairman of a mixed committee dealing with the relations between Pacifism and Revolutionary

movements and nearly lost my few grey in trying to understand people of different nationalities.

The English delegation was the most capable in the conduct of business and indeed I have never worked so hard as during the ten days I was in Zurich in digesting resolutions and drawing them up and generally bossing things. I have a preliminary article in the Labour Leader this week and I shall have a longer one [...] giving some of the chief points of the business discussed.[31]

Robinson refers here to 'no evidence of ill-will between the nations', meaning no ill-will between the women of the nations. There was plenty of ill-will among the delegates, the so-called Peacemakers, the Heads of State (all male) gathered in Paris for the peace negotiations leading to the Treaty of Versailles. In Zurich one of the most dramatic moments of the Congress, which perfectly illustrates this harmony, came on the Saturday morning, 17 May, when a French woman, Jeanne Melin, turned up late and was greeted with an ovation and flowers from the German Lida Gustava Heyman:

> A German gives her hand to a French woman, and says in the name of the German Delegation, that we hope that we women can build a bridge from Germany to France and from France to Germany, and that in the future we may be able to make good the wrong-doing of the men. We women of the world who all feel alike, who want to protect and not to destroy, we shall always understand one another.[32]

Jeanne Melin gave an impassioned response and the incident ended with a *Pledge to Work for Peace*:

> Emily Balch [an American pacifist] stood, and raising her hand, invited all present to join her in pledging themselves to do everything in their power towards the ending of war and the coming of permanent peace.[33]

The eagerly-awaited Treaty of Versailles brought more than disappointment. It brought despair, making, as it did, reconciliation between the nations of Europe impossible 'with the greed-inspired lie ... that the whole guilt of the war rested upon one nation who ... should be forced to pay the whole cost'.[34] Germany's economy was left

Margaret Macmillan asks: "How can we outlaw war?" This WILPF supporter has an answer: Disarmament

in ruins: by punishing Germany so harshly 'the peace-makers' in effect made the Second World War inevitable.

But taking the long view the situation could be seen as more nuanced. Margaret Macmillan wrote:

> Of course things might have been different if Germany had been more thoroughly defeated. Or if the United States had been as powerful after the First World as it was after the Second – and had been willing to use that power. If Britain and France had not been weakened by the war or if they had been so weakened that the United States had felt obliged to step in. If Austria-Hungary had not disappeared. If China had not been so weak. If Japan had been more sure of itself. If states had accepted a League of Nations with real powers. If the world had been so thoroughly devastated by war that it was willing to contemplate a new way of managing international relations. The peacemakers, however, had to deal with reality, not with what might have been. They grappled with huge and difficult questions. How can the irrational passions of nationalism or religion be contained before they do more damage. How can we outlaw war? We are still asking those questions ...[35]

It is now widely recognised by historians that the Treaty was never properly enforced: sufficient to anger the German populace, but not enough to prevent the growth of German military power.

WILPF has kept very close to this original object in the century since its foundation. The structure it was given in Zurich – its membership, executive committee, presidency (and the voting system for both), consultation committee and international committee – has stood it in good stead both at national and international level. And WILPF was, essentially, Emmeline Pethick-Lawrence's baby. She saw it through from its conception in the Hague, nurtured it in London during the war years and acted as midwife at its birth in Zurich, full term in 1919 during the conference in Zurich.

Among the foreign delegates in Zurich who Emmeline met was Mary Church Terrell, the African-American civil rights campaigner and suffragist. She came to Zurich from the 2nd Pan-African Congress held in Paris in 1919, one of a series of such meetings (the first one had been held in 1900) which campaigned for peace and decolonization in Africa and the Caribbean. Women played a big part in organising the

Pan-African Congress, but much to their disappointment, it was largely taken over by men, who paid little regard to women's arguments. Mary Church Terrell would have been pleased and relieved to find that the Zurich conference gave women's voices more than enough space.[36]

When it was Terrell's turn to speak in Zurich, she pointed out that as the only woman of colour at the conference, it was her sole privilege to represent, not only the women of colour in the United States, but the whole continent of Africa as well. Her impassioned speech was given greater poignancy by the fact that colonized races from across the world had been fighting, and dying, in the First World War (for example, the French army included around 135,000 Senegalese troops fighting in the trenches of the western front – of whom some 35,000 were killed).[37] Terrell later wrote:

> We believe that no human being should be deprived of an education, prevented from earning a living, debarred from any legitimate pursuit in which he wishes to engage, or be subjected to any humiliation on account of race or colour.[38]

After the Zurich Conference Emmeline spent some time giving talks in Germany to promote a spirit of reconciliation, alongside a French colleague, the journalist and novelist Marcelle Capy. Emmeline went on from Germany to Austria, where the mayor of Salzburg gave her delegation three loaves of bread, symbolic of the lack of food in the country. She attended many public meetings in Germany and spoke of the 'anguish that war brought to women, of the suffering it wrought on disinherited children and of the madness which destroyed the young… men'.[39] She was 'overwhelmed with admiration for the spirited courage in which all…. faced their difficulties and tribulations'. In Vienna she attended gala performances at the opera house, where musicians performed free in times of bread famine.

Her admiration for the Germans and the way they coped with the disaster of defeat was enormous. She was particularly impressed by two German women who had been at the Zurich Conference – Dr Anita Augsburg and Lida Gustava Heymann – and the way they threw themselves into working for reconciliation and peace. Having suffered great privation during the war, these two women took up the task of educating the women of Germany for the new opportunities offered by civic service. They were subsequently to lose their shared house, their passports and everything they possessed when the Nazis came to power, but they continued to fight for the welfare of refugees even after they were themselves driven into exile.

In 1924 Emmeline was invited back to Germany to speak at an international demonstration for peace at the German Reichstag, and she was very roused by the 'passion for peace expressed in these speeches'. Later she was invited by the German President Herr Friedrich Ebert, who undertook the repatriation of war exiles and prisoners after the war, to speak at another peace Conference.

Emmeline remained very loyal to WILPF, serving as its treasurer from 1915 to 1922. After the war she was elected to various positions in women's rights organisations, as well as peace organisations, such as the Women's Freedom League, the Open Door Council and the Six Point Group, the British Feminist Campaign founded by Lady Rhondda in 1921. She still had great hopes for the rights of women and devoted considerable time to fight for them, keeping these, and the fight for peace, high on the agenda.

6. Between the Wars

At the end of the war, and in the inter-war years, Emmeline found her mind turning to her first love: her 'concern for the economic and social advancement of the people who do the heavy and arduous work of the world'.[1] For instance, in 1926 she was elected as president of Charlotte Despard's Women's Freedom League, which had grown out of the WSPU in 1907, in an attempt to provide a more democratic alternative to Mrs Pankhurst's autocratic organisation. Emmeline was subsequently re-elected as its president for nine consecutive years.

The 'undeviating purpose' of the WFL was to 'win complete equality for women,' not only in the political realm (which was achieved in 1928, with the Equal Franchise Act which at last gave the vote to all women on the same terms as men), 'but in the industrial and professional world as well.'[2]

Emmeline was also a vice-president of the Six-Point Group, which 'has been successful in bringing the subject of the position of women throughout the world before the Assembly of the League of Nations'.[3]

The Six Point Group had been set up in 1921 by Lady Rhondda. Its 'Six Point Agenda for Women' read as follows:

1) satisfactory legislation on child assault;
2) satisfactory legislation for the widowed mother;
3) satisfactory legislation for the unmarried mother and her child;
4) equal rights of guardianship for married parents;
5) equal pay for teachers and
6) equal opportunities for men and women in the civil service.

Emmeline was also a member for many years of the executive of the Open Door Council, whose purpose was 'to secure to women complete equality in the economic and industrial spheres'. The council was set up in 1926 by Emmeline, Viscountess Rhondda, and others to press for economic opportunities for women, and to oppose the extension of protective legislation for women, as it debarred them from better paid, if physically dangerous, jobs, for example in mining. This was very much a contested area. The council ran an Equal Compensation Campaign from 1941-43, and an Equal Pay Campaign from 1944, led initially by Emmeline's fellow peace campaigner Chrystal Macmillan:

> The gallant group of women who are affiliated to the
> Open Door International concentrate their entire organ-
> izing upon the effort to secure to women complete
> Equality in the economic and industrial spheres. This
> objective has become the spearhead of women's struggle
> for status as adult human beings and draws down upon
> itself all that is left of active opposition to the movement.[4]

These roles demonstrated the shift in emphasis in the women's movement from the national to the international, and the way in which the women's movement remained strong, if less dramatically so than the 'glory days of the suffrage', in the inter-war years. All of these positions paid tribute to Emmeline's continued commitment to the suffrage and to peace, but none demanded – or received – the same degree of commitment she had given to these causes.

Emmeline did not stand for Parliament again after 1918, as she felt it was better to have one in and one outside the House of Commons within her marriage: but she took a very active part in Fred's seven campaigns to become an MP.[5] In December 1923, when Fred stood triumphantly against Winston Churchill in Leicester West, Emmeline successfully trained the local children to sing (very loudly) a song with the refrain 'Vote, vote, vote for Pethick-Lawrence!' This song proved a great success, and it helped Fred secure a majority of more than 4,000 over Churchill. Emmeline was also very glad to have the opportunity in Fred's 1923 campaign to renew her contacts with the leaders of the Labour Party, which had been strong during the pre-war fight for the suffrage. Nationally, although the Conservatives won the most seats at the 1923 general election, they lost their majority in the House of Commons. A precarious minority Labour government led by Ramsay MacDonald followed until December 1924, when MacDonald had to call another election which was won by the Conservatives in a landslide. Fred did well to hang on by more than 700 votes in Leicester West in 1924: many other Labour MPs lost their seats.

The inter-war period was a time of much foreign travel for Emmeline, in the interests of the 'international unity of women'. She went to the USA twice, to Africa three times, and in 1926 she travelled with Fred to India, where she was in touch 'with the remarkable group of educated and progressive Indian women'. In 1930 she went to South Africa, where white women had just been enfranchised, and to a Congress in Constantinople, where she was immensely impressed by the progress made by Turkish women 'beyond the wonders and fiction of fairy-tale.'[6]

Perhaps Emmeline's most important journey in the inter-war years was much closer to home. In 1921 she went to Ireland, to investigate atrocities committed by the Black and Tans, the forces stationed in Ireland to assist the Royal Irish Constabulary (RIC) to suppress the Irish struggle for national independence (the name 'Black and Tans' comes from the fact that they wore surplus military uniforms).[7] Most of the Black and Tans were unemployed veterans of the First World War. Although they were supposedly members of the RIC, they had no training as policemen and they soon gained a reputation for brutality and wanton destruction. For example, in September 1920 the Black and Tans had burned down twenty houses in Balbriggan, looted pubs and beat two men to death, and on 21 November – known as 'Bloody Sunday' – British forces shot dead 13 civilians at a Gaelic football match at Croke Park in Dublin. In December 1920 came the 'Burning of Cork', in which five acres of the city were badly damaged by fire.

After Emmeline had collected a number of sworn statements about abuses by British soldiers, police officers and 'Black and Tan' auxiliaries she contacted the *Daily News* (in those days the most radical of British newspapers) back in London. On Wednesday 27 April 1921 the front page of the *Daily News* carried a story with Emmeline's byline (alongside another article about guests at a hotel in Castle Connell being fired at by Black and Tans using banned 'dum-dum' bullets, an incident that had been witnessed by a doctor, W Harrison Cripps, and raised in the House of Lords by his brother, the maverick Conservative peer Lord Parmoor).

Although they were given less prominence, Emmeline's allegations were far more serious than those of Cripps. 'A sojourn in Ireland under present conditions is an amazing experience,' her report began. 'Every civilian of British nationality who can by the sacrifice of money or leisure afford to go to Dublin or to any part of Southern Ireland should do so for his own education and enlightenment. Even the casual observer would have a revelation of what a military occupation means when it is enforced upon a hostile civilian population.'

Emmeline's report then recalled a recent stay at an inn in a country village (Macroom, County Cork), where a curfew meant that no lights were permitted to be visible from windows after 7pm. Any civilian on the streets after curfew was in fear of being 'shot on sight'. 'Every night in that small village the inhabitants expect a raid by men armed to the teeth,' Emmeline wrote. 'A few miles distant from this particular spot I talked to women and girls who had been subject to the terror of men with white handkerchiefs covering their faces... Raiding their bedrooms in the dead of night to terrify and insult them'.

Emmeline had spoken to a pregnant woman who had been 'forcibly raped' and whose 'frenzied plea that she expected shortly to become a mother was disregarded'. The woman had seen a priest the following morning, who had advised her to go to a solicitor so her complaint could be raised at police headquarters. Cleverly, Emmeline had also obtained her own sworn statement from the rape victim, as she knew that 'Few Irishwomen would openly confess to having been violated in this way – so traditionally strong is the horror of sexual crime in Ireland'.

Emmeline also said that she had been told by the Child Welfare Society 'in one of Ireland's large cities' of cases of civilians being turned out of their homes at night, and then seeing their homes burned to the ground. In one case, a pregnant woman had pleaded with police officers not to burn the clothes of the baby she expected, only to be beaten with the butt end of their rifles'. The woman and her two young children had then had to wander for miles, in bare feet, before finding somewhere to stay the night.

Emeline's revelations were immediately picked up in parliament, which debated them on Friday 28 April, just two days after they had appeared in the *Daily News*.[8] Sir Hamar Greenwood MP, the Liberal government's Chief Secretary for Ireland, said that having read Emmeline's story he had 'at once wired the Chief of Police and the Commander-in-Chief in Ireland, and told them "Read this and deal with it line by line".' But many MPs, even on the Liberal benches, were sceptical about Greenwood's willingness to properly investigate Emmeline's allegations, or the recent deaths of two men on the streets of Dublin after curfew hour. William Wedgwood Benn (Liberal MP for Leith) exclaimed, 'The Right Honourable Gentleman is unable to find the men who committed these terrible murders. What a record of failure! What a shameful record of disgrace, unequalled in the case of any Chief Secretary who ever sat on that bench!'

Although Greenwood defended the 'gallant forces for which I speak' and insisted that they were keener than anyone 'to wipe out the stigma which some try to attach to them of bring unworthy of the uniforms they wear', Emmeline's account of Irish civilians living in terror of those uniforms made his words ring hollow. Five weeks later, on Monday 6 June, the *Daily News* reported that Emmeline had sent further details of her allegations to the Chief Secretary's office in Dublin Castle, who had assured her that the Lords Justice of Ireland were 'anxious to make the closest investigations into any such allegations'.

In the event the terrible cases of abuse that Emmeline had high-lighted were not followed up by the Lord Justices.[9] But Emmeline's revelations, along with others', had helped to turn public opinion on the mainland against the Black and Tans, and they helped to persuade the government that a negotiated ceasefire was the only realistic way of bringing the two-year Irish war of Independence to an end. Testimony from British visitors to Ireland such as Emmeline during the civil war of 1919-1921 played a crucial role in persuading British politicians that some form of Home Rule was the only sustainable future for Ireland (even Sir Oswald Mosley, who was to become leader of the British Fascists, crossed the floor of the house in protest at the government's policies in Ireland).[9]

On 11 July 1921 a truce was agreed, and in December the Anglo-Irish treaty was signed, paving the way for partition and the declaration of the Irish Free State in 1922, when the Black and Tans were finally disbanded. This was not the end to bloodshed in Ireland by any means: a civil war between Irishmen opposed to partition and those that sup-ported it rumbled on into 1923. But there is no doubt that newspaper reports of abuses by British forces, written by Emmeline Pethick-Lawrence and others, played a significant role in bringing about a swift settlement in Ireland by the end of 1921, without which much more blood would have been spilt.

Looking ahead, Emmeline concluded her memoir (published in 1938) on an optimistic note. She had seen huge improvements in 'the status and living conditions of married working women',[10] so that for example they were no longer punished for failing to care for their chil-dren simply because they were poor. Attitudes to women in the House of Commons had also changed for the better, so that for example when a woman entered the Commons as an MP, fewer eyebrows were raised. The attitude of the adult world towards children also changed. Children, Emmeline mused, used to be seen as 'budding criminals and lunatics who could not be trusted to tell the truth and whose tenden-cies to evil must be closely watched and severely suppressed. All that is altered now.'[11]

In her memoir Emmeline drew on her position as a school manager in elementary schools in St Pancras, one of her many community roles in her youth, to note that the experience of children at school had also changed enormously for the better: she observed that many children would rather be at school than home even if unwell.[12] She also returned to her preoccupation with peace:

Emmeline's report on the war in Ireland was front page news – see the column, top right. The story was taken up by the Daily News, and had a big impact.

'Poverty and unemployment are not evils that affect merely a section of the population in many countries: they have become two outstanding causes of international war. The menace of war hangs like the Damocles' sword over the human race.[13]

But, as we have seen, although her contribution to the peace debate is enormous, it is marked how few commentators and writers on the subject of war share her obsession.

7. Dreamer

'Wild, free, a singer of air, height, depth, beauty and all the rest of it'
– Kathleen Fitzpatrick, quoted in *My Part in a Changing World*, p.89

Right at the end of her autobiography, *My Part In A Changing World*, Emmeline speculates:

> The changes that I have seen in my lifetime have been organic changes brought about by mental and spiritual growth … Often in my life I have been called 'a dreamer'. I have seen many – most – of the dreams of my youth come true. But my dreams of the present outdo them far in scope and splendour. Because I have witnessed a change of heart and a corresponding change in circumstances happen many times, I cherish the dream, which is a faith, that it is going to happen again. And when that dream 'comes true' it will mean an end to war for ever.[1]

Emmeline's life was suffused with spirituality, although she was not really religious in any conventional sense. As a small child she learnt hymns from her beloved cook, Charlotte, and she was taken to church from a very early age, but she was, if anything, puzzled by God. She seems to have inherited her 'religious mysticism' from her adored father, although she only went reluctantly to the various nonconformist chapels he frequented. As her father got older he developed an increasing suspicion of orthodox religion, from which he had torn himself free.

> As he had begun to shed his old beliefs … he was making a cosmogony of his own. He had abandoned the idea of a God of Wrath who had doomed His creation to eternal punishment and could only be appeased by a blood sacrifice. But he could not abandon the mysticism that was part of his Cornish inheritance and which drove him on in his quest for Truth.[2]

A charcoal drawing of Emmeline in the 1930s.
The campaign for women's voting rights continued after the war, despite the
dissolution of the WSPU in 1918.

But Emmeline found her home life in the small seaside town of Weston-super-Mare, what she characterised as 'the most conventional kind of environment to be found – the petty life of a second-rate seaside resort',[3] very confining until she managed to escape to the West London Mission. We saw in Chapter One how it was through her friends and her trips away that she achieved any sense of freedom and transcendence, and she began to hope for real social change. For Emmeline, spirituality was always linked with social justice, as it was closely allied to the natural beauty of the physical world: 'It was a wonderful thing at that period to be young among young comrades… all life lay before us to be changed and moulded by our vision and desire'.[4]

A trip to Cornwall in around 1892, with three female friends, took on an almost mystical, and certainly sentimental, quality :

> I remember very vividly a holiday in Cornwall with three of these boon companions [Ada Vachel, Mabelle Pearse and Kathleen Fitzpatrick], and I never see or think of St Ives without losing consciousness of time, while I live again in these young days. It was in the month of May and the blossoming world was a heaven. The gorse was in full bloom, filling the air with its honey-sweet scent, the hawthorn vied with it in fragrance, the bluebells on the mound rising from the bay were like the deep blue of the sea in colour.[5]

Her hiking holiday in the Swiss Alps with her friend Marie provided several moments of near-ecstasy:

> An hour or two before dawn we all set out together for the last part of the climb. We were in great good luck, for when we reached the summit we were rewarded by the most magnificent sun-rise that I have ever seen. On this particular morning we were more struck by the difference in the aspect of everything in the world, as well as in our own mood, before and after the rising of the sun. On those mountain expeditions we realized afresh that with the reappearance of the sun the world was re-created every day. That morning I remember how the dew sparkled on the grass and flowers, and how the air was like nectar and how light and springing was our step as we returned to our hut for breakfast.[6]

Her great friend, Kathleen Fitzpatrick, urged on her the life of a dreamer:

> There are workers by the score appealing to the people rich and poor from a humanitarian point of view. It is on the other side we want you now. We want poems telling of impossible things – anything that can lift us out of the complacent satisfaction of settlement life, Sisterhoods and the like rot. Chuck it, old lady … follow your own bent and be what you were made to be, and you will do what no one will do, if you leave it undone. Be your own old self, wild, free, a singer of air, height, depth, and all the rest of it. That is your place old lady. Up you go to the top of the mountain and think and think…[7]

But in the event Emmeline's spiritual and emotional needs were not fully met by her young comrades, but by a man 25 years her senior, Mark Guy Pearse, whom she had known in childhood and met up with again in London. Emmeline's childhood relationship with this family friend became 'the supreme influence in my life for the next twenty years,'[8] and 'looking back on my life… it seems as though he actually created in me a new spirit that was part of himself'.[9] While she inherited a belief in justice and freedom from her father, the other massive influence in her early life, Pearse, was 'a believer in one power only, the power of love – a man who hated conflict in any shape or form and always avoided it'.

Emmeline was torn between the contrasting philosophies of these two powerful father figures (she actually referred to Pearse in her letters as 'the Daddy'):

> When confronted with injustice and cruelty, my instinct is a militant one, I want to challenge evil and fight with all the powers of mind and body, and yet I recognise the truth that the power of love is alone strong enough to solve all problems and remove all oppressions.[10]

Mark Guy Pearse had helped his friend Hugh Price Hughes to establish the West London Mission in 1887. Their styles were very different. Price Hughes was 'a man of fiery temperament and dominating force; a born challenger and fighter',[11] while Pearse was a man who loved peace and hated conflict, who turned as a child to Mother Nature. But their skills complemented each other. Their partnership

Mark Guy Pearse

meant that Emmeline was thrown together with Pearse again when she went to London, and he took a great interest in the work of the 'sisters', supporting them with money as well as sympathy. Emmeline went to hear Pearse preach from the platform of St James's Hall, a concert hall off Piccadilly that had been designed by Owen Jones and opened in 1858, where his oratory 'opened … the doors of vision to his listeners [and]… poured the balm of consolation into wounded and broken hearts'.[12] Her relationship with Pearse developed into one of comrade-ship and union in a common purpose, although it nearly faltered when she told him of her plan to move away from the West London Mission, with Mary Neal, and set up on their own. Mark's displeasure at this was only assuaged when Emmeline burst into tears with the words 'You have never been cold to me before – and – you see – *I love you so*'.[13] Their relationship was restored, and Pearse became a great supporter of the two young women and continued to provide Emmeline with an 'all-sufficing friendship'. This relationship was characterised by a 'sense of oneness that deepened as we shared our experience of thought and life', and Emmeline credited it with her faith in life as fundamentally joyous (although there is no doubt it crosses the line into sentimentality).

When Emmeline met Fred Lawrence, Pearse was one of first to recognise Fred's qualities and he officiated at their wedding in 1901. The subsequent cooling in her relationship with Pearse apparently had nothing to do with her marriage. Instead it was seriously undermined by Emmeline and Fred's subsequent involvement with the militant suffrage movement:

> He was distressed. Like many others, though not opposed to the principle of women's political equality, he regarded militancy with extreme distaste and profoundly regretted my association with it. He showed great forbearance but when our behaviour grew from bad to worse, he wrote me a letter to tell me that our friendship could no longer continue. I threw it in the fire…[14]

Emmeline was reconciled with Mark Guy Pearse in his old age, after the militancy of the suffragettes was abandoned, and she fully acknowledged the lifelong debt she owed him: 'This enduring friendship begun in childhood, with a man so gifted and so good, could not fail to be a dominant influence in my life,' she later wrote.[15]

Reading about it more than 80 years later, Emmeline's relationship with Pearse seems over-intense, controlling, and possibly unhealthy (Mark Guy Pearse certainly awoke 'a passion of love and admiration' in several other children, Emmeline says). At best it would appear to be a sort of teenage 'crush' that was extended into adulthood. It does not appear to have been overtly sexual, although of course it could have been. Yet Pearse clearly fulfilled her need for powerful, charismatic figures to give purpose to her life.

Emmeline certainly, as we saw, found spiritual support and inspiration in the suffragette movement: 'A new absorbing interest had taken possession of my mind and was demanding all my emotion and energy.

I was pledged to the loyalties of a revolutionary movement.[16] She saw this in almost transcendental terms:

> to us had been committed the power of the Creative Thought: the 'Word' that would not return to the spiritual realm, void. The conviction that took possession of me then, never left me again. I realised that the Creative Thought had descended from the spiritual realm down into the human mind, had possessed the reason and the emotions and had passed finally into the blood and had thus become a power in the physical world.[17]

Undoubtedly way 'over the top' but it clearly fulfilled a great need for Emmeline.

We saw in Chapter Three how the charismatic, autocratic Emmeline Pankhurst (a woman 'of destiny... like some irresistible force in nature – a tidal wave or river in full flood),[18] and other top members of the WSPU inspired in Emmeline extraordinary reserves of courage, oratory and amazing organisational and fund-raising skill, all for a cause in which she believed passionately. Speaking at Caxton Hall in 1908, she said she felt inspired by spiritual powers, and that 'it was no power of my own that prevailed'.[19]

Emmeline was to explore other roads to enlightenment, including the spiritual path provided by the Baha'i religion, established in 1844 by the Báb in Iran, and which later became fashionable in Europe and the United States. She was probably attracted by its intense spirituality and also because, like the Unitarians, the Baha'i believe in the unity of all religions and that God has sent humanity a series of messangers to educate humanity and advance civilization: human society needs a unifying vision of the nature and purpose of life.

In 1911 the then-leader of the Baha'i Faith, Abdu'l-Baha, made a trip to Europe, and spoke to huge audiences bearing his father's message on 'how to build a new civilisation based on spiritual peace, justice and unity to a western audience'.[20] Suffragettes were among those who turned up at these meetings. In London he stayed with Lady Blomfield, and it was in her house that he first met Emmeline Pethick-Lawrence.

Emmeline was in tune with Abdul Baha's thinking, especially on equality between men and women and on peace, and she was able to contribute to his thinking as well as learn from it. At one of their meetings where the suffrage issue was raised, he elaborated on his metaphor of humanity being like a bird with two wings, men and women. Humanity's flight would be hampered if one wing was stronger than the other. After this encounter Abdu'l-Baha adopted this metaphor of the bird with two wings as his signature image of equality between man and women.[21]

Abdu'l-Baha consistently expressed support for the suffragette movement, though he was vehemently against violence or militancy. And he spoke out constantly against war and in support of universal peace, in the hope that "'a bond of unity and agreement may be estaboished between the East and west...'"[22]

This would have further appealed strongly to Emmeline, who was about to be forced to abandon her life as a suffragette for that of an ardent peace campaigner, against the unfolding horrors of the First World War.

However, the Baha'i faith ith its many prohibitions was a strange religion for a very independent, socially-liberal woman, and a progressive feminist from a non-conformist Christian background, to be attracted to. Once again, Emmeline's attraction to it seems to have been, at least in part, due to the presence of charismatic men.

Emmeline invested the fight for peace with the same passion that she had invested the fight for votes. She attended the Peace Conference in the Hague in 1915 and was very active in the Zurich Congress in 1919. She found that much that happened in Zurich, particularly the grim news from the official Peace conference in Paris – in such stark contrast to the promotion of world peace to which the women in Zurich were dedicating themselves – reduced her to tears. She felt that the conference was 'perhaps the most moving experience of my life'[23] and she felt remarkable empathy with the women and children in Germany, and refugees, who had suffered the devastation of war, and with the women who had gone to Zurich with her. She felt she was seeing things from a different, clearer, more exalted perspective:

> Here, from these wonderful heights, here in this clearer atmosphere, we get a wider view of humanity than we could isolated in our own country, and looking out upon things from this point of view, we see that war is not only a great world tragedy, the greatest calamity that can come to the human race, we can see that war is the supreme folly, war is the great madness.[24]

This passion, as we have seen, informed all her contributions to the

Zurich Congress, and carried over into her work for peace after 1919, much of it in Germany.

The 1920s saw Emmeline involved with John Hargrave, another autocratic and charismatic leader: this time of a youth movement, the Fellowship of the Kibbo Kift. The Kibbo Kift had been set up in 1920, 12 years after the establishment of the Boy Scout (and the Girl Guide) movements. Hargrave had been part of the Scout movement himself, until he left it after becoming disillusioned with the Scouts' militaristic leadership. Unlike these organisations, Kibbo Kift was open to both sexes, and welcoming to all classes. Hargrave saw it as a movement,

> that would break down social and sexual barriers, leading the nation to physical and spiritual regeneration, and his advocacy of social relevance and the regeneration of urban man through the open-air life was a sentiment with which social reformers like Emmeline and Mary Neal could identify.[25]

A Kibbo Kift gathering in the grounds of Emmeline's house in the Surrey Hills.

The Kibbo Kift (which apparently means 'proof of strength' in Cheshire dialect) was founded by Hargrave and other pacifists to promote creative expression, physical health and fitness through camping, hiking and handicrafts – and to produce 'hard bodies and straight thinking' in response to the horrors of the First World War. In the 1920s it attracted figures like H G Wells and D H Lawrence, but it only ever had a tiny membership: no more than a few hundred at any one time, and perhaps 2,000 overall.

Despite its small size, its 'spiritual seekers, life reformers, educators and dreamers' wished nothing less than to fashion a new world, with the help of dress and self-presentation. Sartorial appearance was a core part of the Kibbo Kift project. Its leaders developed an original and idiosyncratic aesthetic across all aspects of their dress, art, craft and design, summed up in the phrase 'picturesqueness in everything'. Their passion for world reforms was addressed in terms of reverence for the body, while group costumes ranged from the practical to the dramatic. Their outlandish, and sometimes self-consciously ridiculous, costumes communicated their radical distinctiveness and their wholesale rejection of 'civilised' culture and dress (with the bowler hat the greatest target of Hargrave's scorn). This fed into the thinking of the Men's Dress Reform Party of the 1920s, in which comfort and practicality were emphasised. The Men's Dress Reform Party may sound like something out of a Monty Python sketch, but it did in fact exist, and took itself very seriously.

There was a lot in the Kibbo Kift that attracted Emmeline; its commitment to young people, the opportunity (at the beginning, at least) for women's leadership, its emphasis on peace and brotherhood, and its 'reverence for folklore and pageantry, and belief in the power of the countryside'.[26] She threw herself into the movement with great enthusiasm, giving it support and money, sitting on its council, and even taking the tribal name 'Lototsa' ('looking towards the stars'). She hosted the Kindred's Second Althing (annual 'meet') at her home in London in 1921, and made her house and grounds in Surrey available for the Kibbo Kift's camps (many of then led by John Hargrave in the guise of 'White Fox'), hikes and other outdoor activities. She also tried to use her contacts to connect the Kibbo Kift with European youth groups.

The Kibbo Kift's elaborate cultural activities included spiritual ritual, shamanism and mysticism as well as original theatre and song, linking performance art with cutting-edge design and public spectacle (Hargrave had worked in advertising earlier in his life, so he would have understood the importance of presentation). The role of beauty in Kibbo Kift also linked to their particular approach to gender and sexuality. Women should do their utmost to be attractive, well-dressed and graceful. The organisation's conformist attitudes to sex roles and relationships led eventually to gendered ideas about leadership, with little role for women. Nietzschean ideas about human perfectibility, although denied by the organisation, undoubtedly underpinned much of Kibbo Kift's thinking about bodily beauty and sexual behaviour.

The Kibbo Kift's concern with physical fitness, the culture of beauty and the propagation of a new, healthy generation echoes some aspects of the eugenic ideal, which circulated among a wide range of reformers across the political spectrum who were in search of social betterment in the early decades of the twentieth century. Eugenics were, of course, later taken up by national fascist regimes, with catastrophic consequences.

It is worth noting that Emmeline had a brush with eugenics in the 1920s, when she was attracted by the work of the birth control pioneer Marie Stopes, and she spent part of the 1920s and 1930s involved in Stopes' campaign to provide information about birth control to working class women. In the nine decades since Stopes has aroused much controversy for her establishment of a 'Society for Constructive Birth Control and Racial Progress', and her avowed opposition to 'reckless breeding' by 'the semi-feebleminded [and] the careless'. Stopes, a palaeobotanist before she became a pioneer birth control campaigner, was a guest at Fourways (the house near Peaslake, Surrey, that the Pethick-Lawrences had built in 1921) and Fred wrote her a letter of introduction when she went to India. Emmeline contributed an article by an old friend Havelock Ellis to Stopes' *Birth Control Review*,[27] and her name appeared on the list of the society's supporters on its printed notepaper, along with those of Lady Constance Lytton and the feminist novelist Vera Brittain. Stopes' society was of course the Society for Constructive Birth Control and Racial Progress. With hindsight it seems shocking that Emmeline should associate herself with a society that endorsed 'racial progress', with all the racist connotations that now carries. Professor Mary Joannou, who sorted through boxes of Marie Stopes papers at the Welcome Institute in the late 1980s and early 1990 was 'appalled by some of Stopes's eugenicist and racist attitudes which need to be understood in the context of her time'.[28] One might argue it was more an error of judgement on Emmeline's part than of deeply held belief. Emmeline's interest in Marie Stopes seems to have tailed off as the years passed, although in 1950 her name still appeared as a Vice President of the associated Mother's Clinic in Whitfield Street. This is clearly a difficult area as Marie Stopes is also a feminist hero for her introduction of birth control particularly to poor women.

For such a small organisation, the Kibbo Kift certainly had grandiose ideas to change the world, its global goals in 1920 being, rather bizarrely, to bring about 'international educational policy', 'international freedom of trade', an 'international currency system',' the abolition of secret treaties' and the 'establishment of a World Council of every civilised and primitive nation or race'.[29] Annabelle Pollen has argued that the Boy Scout Movement produced a little-known offshoot of 'intellectual barbarians, whose charismatic leader had dreams of overcoming the existing crises of the twentieth century'.[30] But the Kibbo Kift had neither the time nor the opportunity to achieve its lofty goals (even if they had been achievable), as the organisation existed in its original form for little more than a decade. During its short life, it was a very 'top-down' organisation, with many internal upheavals. In response to the economic problems of the late 1920s, Hargrave transformed his 'Kindred' into a more politico-economic movement. The singing, hiking, flowing cloaks, and mystical ceremonies by firelight gave way to marching and military-style uniforms.[31] By the 1930s it had transformed into the Green Shirt Movement for Social Credit, and in 1931-2 into the Social Credit Party of Great Britain, which was finally wound up in 1951. It is important to remember that John Hargrave's Green Shirt movement was not in any way analogous to the fascist Black Shirts: indeed in the 1930s it engaged in street battles with Oswald Mosley's British Union of Fascists. In any case, as far as is known Emmeline severed all connection with what had been the Kibbo Kift in the 1920s, and she had no links with its later manifestations.

Despite its small size, the Kibbo Kift left something of a legacy – including a major book by Annabelle Pollen, a number of articles, two exhibitions at the Whitechapel Art Gallery (in 1929 and 2015-6,) a rock musical in 1976 and a major archive collection in the LSE Library. It gave inspiration to a number of artists, and most lastingly it inspired the left wing youth movement the Woodcraft Folk, which grew out of the Kibbo Kift in 1925 and exists to this day.

John Hargrave had been very much in the same mould as Emmeline's other charismatic spiritual muses, such as Mark Guy Pearse, the Baha'i Religion, the peace movement, and other forms of spiritual comfort: her family reported that in the late 1920s she was having horoscopes done, and some of these have survived amongst her papers.[32] But in the end the person who gave her the most sustained spiritual and emotional support was not a flamboyant outsider, but the person closest to her: her husband Fred.

However far Emmeline travelled, both geographically and spiritually, her marriage remained at the core of her life. Fred remarked on Emmeline's 'deep spiritual' quality after only their second meeting, and this quality, along with deep devotion, informed the whole of their subsequent relationship.

In 1904 Emmeline wrote to Fred from Egypt where she was on holiday with friends:

> Beloved,
>
> I scarcely know how to sit down and write to you tonight. My heart is too full. I could sit still for hours wrapt in a garment of joy. Ever sense satisfied to the uttermost – one's whole being steeped in sensation. Nothing has ever been the least bit like it – light and colour and wonder. I don't think I have ever felt so splendidly well, so vitalized, so filled with life… But can only tell you this – there is something here that is different from anything I have ever known though it is something I have guessed at – dreamed of – there is something here that is fills one's mind with light and glory – and calls new things into being.[33]

More than forty years later, Emmeline wrote to Fred from Lincoln's Inn, where he was packing to go to India (they often exchanged notes within the flat). The letter has a pantheistic tone:

> We share our deepest attitude to life and being. To some at any rate, like the Buddhas in Tibet, we have found our being outside the wheel of Birth and Death. Outside or inside we know we are part of the Cosmic whole, and to the extent of our realisation, are beyond anxiety or fear. If only we two…. Involved in the great enterprise of reconciliation can live … in this consciousness, the 'Miracle' may happen. I have always felt that the marvellous outpouring of what we call the Holy Spirit at Pentecost was due (in part at any rate) to the sudden consciousness of oneness generated by the vigil together, and to the realization of what St Paul in his great chapter in Corinthians called 'Charity' – Understanding – Fellowship – oneness – so that all spoke in language understood of every tribe and nation.[34]

Fred replied from Delhi:

> My spirit has not flagged. Your noble words written
> before I left, to the effect that in a measure you and I had
> already escaped from the wheel of life and death have
> come to me from time to time. Your love token bearing
> witness to our relationship to the central life is with
> me...[35]

But the greatest token of love which Fred wrote for Emmeline was
a poem, 'A Song of Spring', which described the flowers in the garden
at Fourways. The poem was written in the spring of 1930, while
Emmeline was away on a visit to South Africa.

A SONG OF SPRING

I saw the snowdrops, stars of winter's night,
And asked who gave them courage to upraise
Their shapely heads, and hide them not in fright
At cold and biting winds in earth's dark days.
They answered "She who gave us life's delight
 Enjoined on us to gladden all your ways;
For love of her we smile at frost despite."

...

But to the wild, wild rose, the rose of June,
Mine own full song of ecstasy I'll sing;
"Thy heavenly colours draw from sun and moon,
From love's sweet breath thy honeyed fragrance bring,
Weave texture from th' ethereal air at noon,
Transcend in loveliness, all flowers of Spring,
For my dear love comes home to me in June.[36]

This poem was probably written with 26 May in mind – this had
been a significant date in Fred and Emmeline's courtship, which they
celebrated throughout their marriage: they were always very keen on
anniversaries. The feeling of spiritual intensity in her relationship with
Fred did not lessen over the years, nor did his for her. Whether their
marriage was celibate or not, it was undoubtedly devoted and spirituality was integral to that devotion.

Emmeline and Fred had no children, as Emmeline was unable to

Emmeline with "her family" of children [Museum of London]

have children after an early miscarriage. But they were both (and especially Emmeline) devoted to children and young people, and they both
lavished care on them – from the Esperance Girls, to the little girls
from Ireland, to Sylvia Pankhurst's son Richard, and to older girls like
Christabel Pankhurst and Annie Kenney, whom they treated like
daughters (like Christabel, Annie spent much time living with the
Pethick-Lawrences in London, and at The Mascot). Emmeline put a
lot of energy into providing holidays for poor children by the sea at the
Green Lady Hostel, and through the Children's Country Holiday
Fund. The Sundial was designed with children in mind, and she much
valued her experiences with what she called her 'family': young people
in the Esperance Group and the Kibbo Kift. I have found no reference
at all to any sadness they might have felt by their inability to have their
own children apart from an initial comment by Fred when he first
heard the news of the miscarriage. We can interpret this as we wish.

8. In The Surrey Hills

After their marriage Emmeline and Fred divided their time, when they were not travelling, between a flat in London and a succession of houses in rural Surrey. Their first flat in London was at Clement's Inn: an address which was to become famous for the suffragette movement since it became, in effect, the headquarters of the WSPU.

Clement's Inn stood on the corner of the Strand, next to the Inns of Court. It had been one of the Inns of Chancery until it was 'decommissioned' in 1903, but it had an afterlife as flats and offices, and it is now part of the London School of Economics, which has a hall of residence on the corner of the Strand named Emmeline Pethick-Lawrence Hall. Fred bought, on their first anniversary of their wedding, a separate garden flat for Emmeline, in the same building, to give her some privacy.

The takeover of Clement's Inn by the WSPU was a sort of war of attrition, as more and more rooms were taken over to accommodate its increased activity (and funds). Fred and Emmeline also put people up in their flat there: most notably Christabel Pankhurst, who arrived in 1906 and stayed for the next six years.

The WSPU moved their offices after their split with the Pethick-Lawrences, but Fred and Emmeline stayed at Clement's Inn until it suffered war damage in the First World War, and it was eventually requisitioned by the Air Ministry. As a result Fred and Emmeline had to relocate to two flats at Old Square in Lincoln's Inn in 1917, where they remained, at least during the week, for the rest of their lives. Their two secretaries, Esther Knowles and Gladys-Groom Smith, had to spend much time shuttling between the flats (via 62 steps) with notes which the couple wrote to each other during the day, which is one indication of a very unusual marriage.

Emmeline loved Lincoln's Inn:

> I am fortunate in having a home in London amongst such dignified and beautiful surroundings. The walled garden of Lincoln's Inn with its lawns and old plane trees has given me more tranquillity than my own garden in the country, which keeps my mind and body incessantly active.

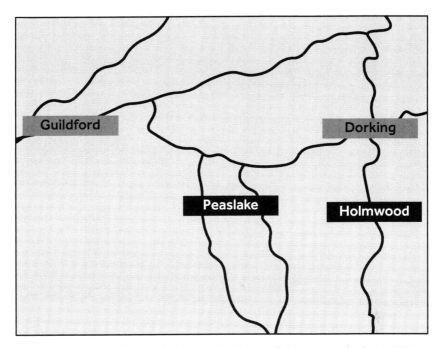

The Mascot and The Sundial were in Holmwood; Fourways, built in 1921,
was in Peaslake. In 1955 Dorking Labour Halls (85 South Street) was
renamed Pethick-Lawrence House in Fred's honour, opened by Clement Attlee.

But their hearts were really in Surrey. Over their lifetime they occu-
pied a number of houses near Guildford, starting with the Dutch
House (a house designed by Edwin Lutyens) at Holmwood, near
Dorking. They bought the Dutch House before their wedding day in
1901, and they moved in soon after and renamed it The Mascot.[3]

The Mascot is a very idiosyncratic house. According to Pevsner, it is
Y-shaped, with rooms radiating in three directions from a central hall-
way. The Mascot stood in eight acres of land and Emmeline would
have seen the potential of the property at once. It was visited by all the
luminaries of the suffragette and socialist movements (including Annie
Kenney, who stayed there for most of 1906, Olive Schreiner, Lady
Constance Lytton, Keir Hardie, George Lansbury, Ramsay
MacDonald and all the Pankhursts: Emmeline, Sylvia and Christabel).
The Mascot's garden even had an outdoor tree platform from which
suffragettes could practise their speeches, and another platform gave
space to sleep out in hot weather.

The Mascot effectively became the weekend headquarters of the
WSPU, and as imprisonment and force-feeding became common, it

Above: The Mascot, designed by Sir Edwin Lutyens, was originally known as The Dutch House. The Pethick-Lawrences moved in in 1901.
[Neville Grant]

Right: The Speech Tree in the Mascot's garden. Suffragettes used to ascend the tree to practise public speaking.
[Neville Grant]

became a place of refuge and recovery after prison, both for Emmeline and many of her suffragette colleagues and friends. Guests were driven down from London, or were met at the station by Mr Rapley, the incredibly discreet chauffeur who stayed with the Pethick-Lawrences for fifty years: before the First World War he drove one of the few motor cars in the neighbourhood. According to the *Daily News*, any attempt to extract information on the suffragettes from Rapley would produce the crushing response 'I don't think'.

Emmeline also set aside a large room at the top of the house as a weekend retreat for the Esperance girls, with whom she had a close involvement during her days as a social worker in London. The girls would come for holidays, and they would on occasion dance at household events, and take part in picnics, croquet games in the garden, local fetes and cricket matches.

Both Fred and Emmeline contributed to local life in Holmwood, by opposing the enclosure of the common opposite their house, and by buying a billiard table for (and donating books to) the local village club. Fred also built himself a billiard room – with spectator space, a bath-

The dormitory for the Esperance girls at the top of The Mascot.
[Neville Grant]

Nearby, the Pethick-Lawrences built The Sundial in 1903 to accommodate a holiday home for women and girls. [Neville Grant]

room and dressing room – alongside The Mascot, which is now a separate house.

In 1903 Emmeline and Fred bought some land to the north of The Mascot, on which they built a holiday home for underprivileged women and children. This came to be known as The Sundial, with a cheerful inscription on its wall: 'Let others tell of storm and showers. I tell of sunny morning hours'.[4] The Sundial included two dormitories, and an inscription in the hallway which read 'In Praise of Mother Earth and of her daughter The Green Lady'. The Sundial's opening ceremony in June 1904 featured someone impersonating a fairy and local children knocking on the door, and Emmeline gave a speech in which she explained how much she appreciated the joy of sharing.

In 1912 Fred and Emmeline Pethick-Lawrence and Christabel Pankhurst found themselves having to bear the cost of the conspiracy trial, and bailiffs arrived at The Mascot, to sell all the contents, as has already been explained in Chapter Four.[5] The house itself was only saved from being forcibly sold by being bought by Emmeline's brother-in-law Thomas Mortimer 'Mort' Budgett, the husband of her sister Annie.

This sale of furniture was challenged by the 'Dorking and Holmwood Campaign' run by two local suffragettes, Charlotte Marsh and Helen Gordon Liddle. Their campaign lasted for six weeks in September and October 1912 and involved rallies and meetings on Holmwood Common, and in local public halls and public houses, to gather support.

By this time the Surrey Hills were increasingly popular as a place for writers, artists and suffragettes to live, who followed in the wake of those who had gone before, and many of them became involved in the campaign.[6] As a result, between 3,000 and 4,000 people, dressed in suffragette colours, attended the sale at The Mascot on October 31 as a show of sympathy. Fred and Emmeline would have felt very boosted by this show of neighbourly support. Fred treated the bailiffs with the utmost courtesy, on the grounds that they were only doing their duty. Emmeline was cheered and waved as she told friends and neighbours that although things they treasured were to be sold, they were bidding for a greater prize and treasure.

Ruth Cavendish-Bentinck, a renowned member of the WSPU, whose famous suffragist lending library eventually found its way to the Women's Library – now part of the LSE's collection – organised friends and relatives to buy back Fred and Emmeline's possessions. Emmeline was so touched that she said later that the presence of so many supporters had made the occasion one of rejoicing rather than one of regret. A tablet with the words 'O Liberty, Thou Choicest Treasure'(which came from a piece of embroidery designed by Sylvia Pankhurst for her mother to work on in prison) was subsequently put up in The Mascot's hall in commemoration of the auction, with the date Oct 31 1912, and the tablet remains there to this day.[7]

Other local, as well as national, campaigns followed – for women's suffrage, particularly until the Representation of the People Act was passed in 1918, in support of the hunger-strikers who had been forcibly fed; a campaign for Indian Independence – with which Fred was becoming increasingly involved, and collecting funds for Belgian refugees after the start of the First World War. More controversially, some militants organised arson attacks on local houses – including one being built for Lloyd George – although the Pethick-Lawrences were not involved.

Emmeline loved The Mascot's garden, which she wrote about while in Holloway after 1906, and it played an increasingly important role as she spent more time in the country after her release. But in 1921 the Pethick-Lawrences sold the house and the land when increased traffic on the A24 took away its tranquillity. The Sundial was also sold in

Fourways, their house in Peaslake.

1921, to the journalist and war correspondent John Landon-Davies, a prolific writer on history, politics and science, who was involved in the International Brigade in Spain.[8] The Pethick-Lawrences then bought a piece of land between Shere and Peaslake about five miles away on which to build a labour-saving 'cottage' and lay out a two-acre garden. They moved into the new house, named Fourways, in 1921. In the 1920s the land around Fourways was used by the folk dancers of the Kibbo Kift movement.[9] It was also shared with many others. An iconic photograph of Emmeline and Fred at its garden gate was taken in 1949, and used by them as a Christmas card.

There were times when Emmeline could be very irritating, even demanding, but she remained much loved, and she was a very good employer. Interviews which Brian Harrison conducted in the 1970s with surviving suffragettes, and with those who had worked for the Pethick-Lawrences, gave a very clear picture of life at Fourways. Harrison interviewed a number of people who had known Emmeline and Fred from the 1920s, among them were Gladys Groom-Smith, who started to work for the Women's International League in 1922 and then moved to work for Emmeline in 1924. Gladys took on domestic as well as secretarial tasks, but she became Fred's secretary after Emmeline's death, serving until Fred's own death in 1961.

Harrison also interviewed Elizabeth Kempster, who came to

Fourways via an advert for a housekeeper but in effect became Emmeline's nurse and companion, and Nita Needham, the niece of another long-term employee, Esther Knowles, who worked for the Pethick-Lawrences ever since she was recruited to work for Fred at the WSPU offices.[10] Although Esther Knowles had died in 1961 and therefore could not be interviewed by Harrison, Nita had heard a lot from her aunt, who had first come to The Mascot as a little girl (Esther's mother had been an Esperance dancer). Fred had mentioned carrying Esther on his shoulders as a four-year-old.[11] Later, Esther was much helped by Emmeline, moving from being an office girl at the WSPU to become Fred and Emmeline's secretary, managing their personal affairs with great discretion and total commitment. Esther had great intelligence and an ability to get on with those of all ages. Esther considered Emmeline to be her 'lode-star', and was devoted to both of them. When she worked as Fred's parliamentary secretary she habitually dosed herself with anti-migraine medication from a pharmacy on Chancery Lane so she could complete the typing-up of his parliamentary speeches.

All those who worked for the Pethick-Lawrences seemed to share the same commitment and affection for their employers, and a willingness to concentrate on their many good points rather than their irritating faults, which were many. Gladys Groom-Smith recalled that Fred was very keen to promote his employees' self-improvement.

The recordings of Brian Harrison's interviews depict a couple who had great respect for each other's independence, but who were also lonely at times, however brave they might appear in public. They seemed to have never really recovered from being thrown out of the WSPU by Mrs Pankhurst.

In her youth and middle-age Emmeline seems to have enjoyed robust good health. She survived six prison stays and she enjoyed many vigorous trips around the world, whether working (such as to the US in 1914) or on holiday (she went to Egypt in 1904, and on many other trips with Fred). But as she entered her sixties in the 1930s her health began to deteriorate. The first casualty was her hearing. In 1935 she had to turn down an invitation to the All-India Women's Conference because of her deafness,[12] which clearly impinged on Fred: in 1937 his long correspondence with Viscount Robert Cecil on affairs of state was interrupted by discussion on the merits of a particular hearing aid. As a result, Emmeline began to spend more time in Surrey rather than in Lincoln's Inn, because she found it more difficult to cope in London, and her trip to the United States with Lady Rhondda in 1937,[13] on behalf of the Six Point Group, to raise the issue of the position of women throughout the world at the League of Nations, was probably her last foreign trip.

During the 1920s and 1930s Emmeline continued to work assidu-ously for the women's movement, particularly for the Women's Freedom League (of which she was vice-president from 1926 to 1935). In 1928 Emmeline hosted a victory breakfast at the Hotel Cecil in London, on behalf of the WFL, to celebrate the granting of the vote on equal terms with men. But while she retained a keen interest in the movement and kept in touch with many ex-colleagues and friends, the time and energy she could give diminished from the 1930s onwards. Emmeline's life became much quieter. Gladys took on cooking duties at Fourways and began nursing Emmeline in her old age. Gladys's duties at Fourways often took precedence over visits to her husband in Birmingham. As she said to Brian Harrison 'I made *them* my life… simply because I was happy being with them … I don't know how I ever had the time to get married, really'.[14]

9. Towards India

After the start of the First World War Emmeline became a peace campaigner, but her career never again reached the heights of her involvement in the suffragette movement. Meanwhile, however, Fred, encouraged by Emmeline, went on to have a very distinguished career as a Labour politician, firmly within the mainstream of the party. After several failed attempts he was elected to parliament twice.

He was first elected in Leicester West in 1923 (where he defeated Winston Churchill, who had lost his Dundee seat at the general election of November 1922). Fred's maiden speech in 1924 was on the subject of pensions for widowed mothers (a subject close to Emmeline's heart). He was very happy in his five years as a backbencher (until he became a minister in 1929), calling the House of Commons the centre of his life.

Fred lost his Leicester seat in 1931 but he stood again, in 1935, for Edinburgh East, and was elected with a slim majority of just over 1,000. Fred was re-elected there with a much larger majority of 6,500 in the landslide election of 1945, but stood down as Edinburgh East's MP later that year when he was elevated to the House of Lords.

Fred served as Financial Secretary to the Treasury 1929-1931, where he drew Labour closer to Keynesian remedies for unemployment, and he defined politics very broadly to include the health, education and happiness of a nation's human capital.[1] In the autumn of 1931 Fred was invited to take part in the second session of the Round Table Conference, which was dealing with the federal structure of India, shortly before he lost his seat in the general election of October 1931. After returning to parliament in 1935 he was made a privy councillor in 1937, and for a few weeks in January and February 1943 he even served as leader of the opposition – a largely honorary and ceremonial post in wartime, because Clement Attlee, the Labour leader, was deputy Prime Minister in the coalition government.[2]

Fred always maintained a keen interest in the machinations of the Indian sub-continent in the 1930s and early 1940s, and he spoke often about it in the House of Commons, for which he 'gained increasing respect for the breadth of knowledge and sympathy he displayed in the debates on India.'[3] He was thus the obvious choice to be appointed,

Fred and Gandhi. Fred had great admiration for Mahatma Gandhi, whose campaign for India's independence from British rule helped to inspire movements for civil rights and freedom across the world.

after Labour's victory in 1945, as Secretary of State for India and Burma (today's Myanmar). Fred was ideally suited for his new job, although he was characteristically modest about his qualifications for it.

He had first visited India in 1897, but admits that at that time 'my knowledge was nearly all second-hand and my impressions were mostly superficial.'[4]

Nevertheless, when some years later Fred's involvement in the suffrage movement brought him into contact with Mahatma Gandhi, he knew he had met a fellow spirit. Gandhi had been involved in his own non-violent resistance campaign in South Africa, and he was interested in the tactics being employed during the suffrage campaign in England. Recalling Gandhi's visit for lunch (raisins and milk) with him and Emmeline in their flat in London in a radio broadcast in September 1954, Fred said, 'We found we had much in common, not least in his doctrine that a willingness to endure suffering was a surer way to win political reform than to inflict it on others'.[5]

As a Labour MP in the 1920s Fred 'gained increasing respect in Parliament for the breadth of knowledge and sympathy he displayed in the debates on India', his obituary in *The Times* in 1961 recalled. On a silver honeymoon visit to India in 1926-7, he and Emmeline had met many people, including Swarajists who explained Gandhi's campaign to revive India's home industries.[6] During their visit they noted that a large number of women took part in elections for local Legislative Councils, and Emmeline recorded that 'Everybody apparently agrees that the women of this country are developing with astonishing rapidity'.[7] During their visit they met Hindus and Muslims, in many parts of India, including Bombay, Mysore, Darjeeling, Peshawar, the Khyber Pass and Calcutta. Among those who Fred met was Rabindranath Tagore, the Nobel-prize winning poet. In Madras they visited a village where a local tribe had been weaned off *dacoity* (robbery) by providing them with a water source.[8] Fred commented that it showed 'once more that the roots of crime are ignorance and poverty'. Fred also visited the Viceroy, Lord Irwin, and he told him what he had heard about India's desire for self-government. Between the wars, Fred took part in several round-table conferences on the future of India, during which he gained an insight into the issues involved, and some of the personalities.

As Secretary of State for India from 1945 onwards, with a seat in the Cabinet, Fred was faced with a hard task. In a nutshell, the problem was, in his own words, that 'In face of our determination to emancipate India from British rule, we were confronted with political deadlock.

Gandhi had lost faith in British intentions about Indian freedom, [and] Jinnah had lost faith in fair treatment of Moslems at the hands of a Hindu 9 On New Year's Day 1946 Fred broadcast to India in a radio address that 'he felt... he would like to speak personally to the Indian people, and assure them that the British Government and people earnestly desired to see India rise quickly to the full and free status of an equal partner in the British Commonwealth'.[10]

In 1946 Fred led a high-level Cabinet Mission (alongside Sir Stafford Cripps, President of the Board of Trade, and A V Alexander, the first Lord of the Admiralty) to Delhi, in an attempt to identify a smooth way for Indian independence. Fred's stay in India in the run-up to independence kept him away from Emmeline for long periods in 1945-47. Although we have Fred's letters to Emmeline from India, which reflect on his experience there, we do not have any insights in his biography, since his book *Fate has been Kind* ends in 1942. However, it is clear that their relationship remained strong, and helped to sustain Fred in a very stressful period in his life. A number of their letters stored in the Wren Library in Trinity College Cambridge have survived – they wrote to each other almost daily (his letters always signed 'Boy'). Of course, with the inevitable delays it was hard to maintain a dialogue, and letters usually crossed. These quotations give some indication of how close they remained, how Fred had to adapt to a new place – and a new role, and how difficult the ongoing negotiations were:

> My dear
> I have just arrived after a perfect journey. It is an entirely novel experience for me to be a "great" personage & to be received everywhere with the state befitting my position. But it doesn't embarrass me any more than it would to peel potatoes with a cottager's wife… New Delhi, March 24 1946)

> My Dear
> I am now nearing the end of my second day here & tomorrow we are migrating to our private residence in Willingdon crescent. Though everyone has been more than kind here I shall not be sorry to shake off the excessive for-mality & ceremony. At lunch and dinner there are as many servants in gorgeous red livery as there are diners. When the Viceroy & his wife walk into dinner, his own sister and daughter have to curtsey to them … March 25 1946

My Dear
   Since I wrote to you last my days have been more and more crowded up with engagements & I have had very little time to myself. We have been getting down to the main task of the mission ... New Delhi March 28 1946

Dearest
   It has been a very great pleasure to me to get your letter dated March 23 to hear all your news about golf & the garden ... March 30th 1946

Fred's letters inevitably get shorter as the pressure increases. On April 2 he wrote:

Darling
   A brief line in the middle of a v busy week. A delightful talk with Gandhi last night. Nothing definite but just the establishment of mutual goodwill. He specially asked me to send you greetings ...

How 'Boy' found time to write these letters is amazing, given how busy he was. It is clear that he really needed to keep in close touch with his wife. He wrote this on April 3:

My Dear
   We are in the thick of it. Yesterday we started interviews at 10 AM & finishing at 5 went on to a social gathering of the Press (off the record) which lasted 1¾ hours of which one hour I answered questions. This was followed by dinner in our house with 3 prominent Moslem League supporters. The conversations lasted till 11.30 pm during which I had to break off to have a ¾ hour talk with an emissary from Gandhi... I am to have dinner with Jinnah tonight...

Clearly, then, it was a hard road: after a week of intense negotiations in Simla, without any agreement being reached, Fred drafted an Interim Constitution that attempted to achieve a compromise between unity and partition. Gandhi described the document as 'the best that the British government could have produced in the circumstances.' Writing in the Indian newspaper *Harijan*, Gandhi noted that 'It reflects

our weakness, if we could be good enough to see it… We would griev-
ously err if, at this time, we foolishly satisfy ourselves that the differences are a British creation The Congress and the League did not,
could not, agree'.[11]

The good news, for the moment, was that in May 1946 Jinnah's
Muslim League agreed to the Interim Government; the bad news was
that in June the Congress rejected it. After endless negotiations, Fred
agreed a way forward, which was announced by Prime Minister
Clement Attlee in the Commons on 20 February 1947: that the 'British
government intended to transfer power to responsible Indian hands by
a date not later than June 1948'. The Muslim League resolved not to
take part in the planned Constituent Assembly and partition became
inevitable. Amid terrible bloodshed on both sides, Pakistan and India
parted their ways.[12]

In March 1947 the Viceroy of India, Lord Wavell, was replaced by
Lord Mountbatten, and in April, in the midst of rumours that he had
been indecisive, Fred retired as Secretary of State for India. Fred was
now 75, and exhausted. Amidst warm expressions of gratitude on all
sides for Fred's courage and endurance, Lord Listowel took over from
Fred as Secretary of State.

In the end, it must have been some relief to Fred that others became
finally responsible for what followed: the horrors of partition in which
up to two million people killed and millions more were displaced,
amid appalling hardships. Fred was greatly disappointed that he could
not get Hindus and Moslems to agree. He never really managed to
escape the feeling that somehow, he had failed, and he left India a disappointed man. It is ironic – tragic – that a man who in his life was so
dedicated to peace had to leave behind him a situation that led to conflict that continues even up to today.

But even though he was well into his seventies, his commitment to
the relentless process of negotiation with all sides was total. He had
given Indian independence his best shot, and he must claim some
credit for what he achieved. In the words of Dr G P Gooch, in his essay
on Fred 'British Imperialism, sometimes labelled Colonialism, is dead.
Lord Pethick-Lawrence was one of our Elder Statesman who drove the
nails into its coffin'.[13]

Among those who spoke appreciatively about Fred's efforts were
Maulana Abul Kalam Azad, an Indian scholar, Islamic theologian and
independence campaigner. He was a senior leader in the Indian
National Congress during the independence movement – and a
Muslim who believed in a secular state. Like Fred he had experienced
life in prison – he was imprisoned by the British for three years in the

Fred Pethick-Lawrence c. 1910

1940s – and was not even allowed out to attend his wife's funeral.[14] In 1946 he conducted negotiations on behalf of the Congress, assisted by Nehru and Patel. In his book *India Wins Freedom*, published in 1958 shortly before his death, Maulana Azad speaks candidly about some of his fellow politicians (he was very critical of those who favoured partition), and spoke warmly of both Wavell and Pethick-Lawrence, praising their sincerity and uprightness.

The Wren Library at Trinity College, Cambridge also has many letters of appreciation from Indian colleagues and friends, written both before and after his stint as Secretary of State. Sir Stafford Cripps (a member, with Fred, of the Cabinet Mission to India) wrote on the 29 April 1946:

> Your unremitting labour, the high trust in which the Indians held you and your convincing sincerity have created an atmosphere of trust among the Indian people different to anything known since the earliest time of British occupation.[15]

The Wren Library's archive also contains numerous examples of Fred's huge correspondence with politicians, economists, writers and veterans of the women's movement as well as the Indian struggle for independence – Clement Attlee, Hugh Gaitskell, William Beveridge, G D H Cole, John Maynard Keynes, E M Forster, Aldous Huxley, Hugh Dalton, Lord Cecil of Chelwood, the writer and playwright Laurence Housman, Eamon De Valera, Viscount Hailsham, R A B Butler, Victor Gollancz, the East and West Friendship Society, the Inter Parliamentary Union, Louise Garrett Anderson, the prison reformer Margery Fry, the suffragette Evelyn Sharp and her husband, the campaigning journalist and writer H W Nevinson. It also includes correspondence with Christabel and Sylvia Pankhurst – separately of course, since they were seldom on speaking terms. There are also letters from Indira Gandhi, the Mahatma Gandhi Memorial Fund, Jawaharlal Nehru and Indian politicians Krishna Menon, R C Ghose and Amrit Kaur.

Alongside all this discussion of affairs of state with the great and the good, there are many examples of Fred responding generously to requests for help from individuals and organisations – on immigration status, on securing a grace-and-favour apartment, on contributing to a publication, sending money or sending condolences. But he is certainly not a complete push-over and declines, for instance, to help a Mrs Cherian, the Mayor of Madras, to get her daughter into Oxford.

India and Pakistan always remained close to Fred's heart, and after Indian Independence he served as chairman of the East and West Friendship Council. He was also a continuing friend to the women's movement. *Hansard*, the official report of all Parliamentary debates, notes that,

> for the last forty years after the struggle he has given of his great intellect, his money, his time and his energy to women's organisations which have been seeking to open other doors where women might express themselves fully. Pethick-Lawrence was a great gentleman of his generation, and the women of this country have lost a wonderful friend.[16]

Fred and EmmelinePethick-Lawrence

10. The Final Curtain

As she grew older, Emmiline became increasingly reliant on support from a group of devoted servants. Having such a phalanx of people around, both guests and servants, meant she did not have to lift a finger, and increasingly she spent as much time as she needed in bed. Although Emmeline's servants recalled her fondly, they remembered being amazed that she did not know how to wash up dishes. They admitted that their employer could be difficult when Fred went away and left her alone, and that sometimes she could be very self-absorbed. Her staff developed a routine to deal with Emmeline's more difficult moods – for instance Gladys would pat Emmeline's pillow when she needed to wake up. Once Emmeline reached old age, domestic work was delegated to a staff of eight. Brian Harrison, who interviewed surving suffragettes and their employees, notes:

> [She] was quite helpless at domestic tasks. Fred waited on her hand and foot, and always fell for her pleas of illness when there was something she did not want to do. She had the art of surrounding herself with people who doted on her, and she widened the circle of admirers by dictating long letters to relatives. She was a lazy woman who would allow people to do almost anything for her. When she dressed for an occasion she could look rather grand, but often she did not bother. After reading a letter or newspaper she would drop it anywhere, she felt entirely free not to eat a meal that had been carefully prepared for her; she was always losing things and could almost go into trance with a book when reading on her bed, forgetting all her engagements. When she was resting, Gladys was allowed to pat the pillow if interruption was necessary, but nothing more. It says much for her staff's devotion and for Emmeline's charm that the household ran so smoothly, she was not so much selfish as thoughtless, and for all her faults she was nice to work for because she was fun, and treated her employees as individuals, never talking down to them.[1]

This plaque is on the wall outside The Mascot [Neville Grant]

After celebrating her 80th birthday in 1947 Emmeline's health and hearing declined further, particularly after she broke her hip in a fall in the garden in early 1950. Although she was virtually bedridden, she and Fred managed to make it to London to celebrate their golden wedding anniversary in October 1951, with a party at which Sylvia Pankhurst spoke. But it was a heart attack which finally ended her life in on 11 March 1954, aged 86. She died at home in Fourways, with Fred by her side, as she would have wanted.

Fred paid this tribute to Emmeline at her funeral, held at Woking Crematorium, on 14 May 1954:

> All of you have come here because you knew and admired what she did in her public life. But many of you have come also because you were privileged to love her for what was and to be loved by her in return...
>
> She had a great and abiding sense of justice; at whatever

cost to herself she was prepared to resist tyranny At all stages of life she was a champion of the weak against the strong…. Her fight for the equal sovereignty of women is written into the annals of our country's history. She risked her life to call a halt to oppression in Ireland. She loathed war and pleaded for justice for beaten foes. She espoused many lost causes and turned them into winning ones… But of the many victories she won, the greatest of all was the victory over herself – over her and her fears, her limitations and her frailty.

Sylvia Pankhurst, Emmeline's lifelong friend,[2] could not trust herself to attend Emmeline's cremation without distracting tears, as her life partner Silvio Corio had also just died. She wrote to Fred:

> Dear Fred
> I feel you might perhaps think it churlish of me not to have been at the crematorium. But I cannot help crying so much and getting so upset when I care so poignantly that I felt that I should only be a burden to other people…
> I should have been ashamed to go and be a trouble … though would desire to manifest my love and admiration for beloved Emmeline …I have lost one of the pillars of my world, the dearest of long loved friends.[3]

Emmeline Pethick-Lawrence's obituaries appeared in a wide range of newspapers, from the *New York Times* and the *Malay Mail* to the *Dorking Advertiser*, reflecting both the range of her life and yet how she remained rooted in the local. *The Times'* obituarist wrote that Emmeline had been

> A true orator with the great power of inducing sacrifice, a fertile imagination and a great sense of the picturesque. All the colour and pageantry of the militant suffragette movement were due to her efforts. (She did) fine work even before the movement that flamed (her) into incandescence, and her influence continued even after the vote was won. She was indeed in the main stream of Victorian philanthropy but she bought an individual touch and a sense of mission to her work which gave it permanence and something of greatness.[4]

On 9 March 1954 the *Malay Mail* explained:

> Her death ended a great political love story. For over half a century she and her husband fought shoulder in battles for women's rights, for better conditions, for the poor…
>
> Until death split the partnership yesterday they were still hand in hand, a white-haired gentle couple, utterly devoted to each other.

Sylvia Pankhurst, writing in the *Manchester Guardian* on 18 March 1954, did somewhat exaggerate Emmeline's involvement with Ethiopia, which had so dominated Sylvia's later life – she was a great admirer of Haile Selassie and was to move to Addis Ababa in 1956 and die there in 1960. But she wrote with enormous affection that Emmeline had been

> The tenderest and most thoughtful of friends and comrades. In her later years she was still not merely abreast but markedly ahead of her times.

By the time of Emmeline's death in 1954 Fred was a Labour peer in the House of Lords, as Baron Pethick-Lawrence of Peaslake, and although he was now well into his eighties he was still speaking frequently on subjects such as the bank rate and economic growth. Fred was never a great orator, and he was once even dubbed by the press corps as 'Pathetic Lawrence' because of his rather wooden delivery. But in general he was greatly respected for his unusual ability to combine courtesy and moderation with strongly-held views, and his contempt for expediency.

Emmeline had been worried that Fred might be lonely after her death, and she had hoped he would re-marry. In the event he paid her the compliment of choosing to replace her soon as a wife: in 1957 he married Helen Craggs (born 1888), a former suffragette, and one of the first to adopt the tactic of arson, whom he had bailed nearly fifty years earlier. Fred appeared to be happy in his second marriage and Helen outlived him by eight years, dying in 1969.

In spite of having a stroke, which was 'overcome by relentless will power,'[5] after his second marriage, Fred remained an active peer until his death in 1961. He gave his last speech in the House of Lords in July 1961, just a few weeks before his death on 10 September, aged 89. Sadly, he just missed the celebrations for his 90th birthday which the Fawcett Society was planning for December 1961, and to which Fred had been looking forward.

Fred's memorial service was held at St Margaret's, Westminster, on 2 November 1961, and it was packed with the great and the good. But his most moving obituary comes from Theresa Garnett in the December 1961 edition of the little-known *International Women's News* (the newsletter of the International Alliance of Women), which illustrates how his support for the women's cause continued throughout his life:

> He never failed to take up the fight wherever it appeared there was an injustice to women and he was always available to advise and direct us in the best way to present our case.
>
> To those of us who had known him so well in the suffrage days, he was an ever-ready tower of strength and helpfulness. He was always wise, always kind, never mean or revengeful, and we came to regard him with great affection and trustfulness.

The House of Lords devoted time on 17 October 1961 to honour and remember Fred, 'in an atmosphere of emotion usually reserved for those who die in youth'.[6] It is significant that the tribute from Lord Hailsham, for the Government, is as warm and affectionate as that of his Labour colleagues, including Attlee:

> I too noted with a sense of deep respect and admiration, that the noble Lord, who had been a contemporary of my father at school, who so long ago as the South African War had been an outspoken critic of Government policy, and long before the First World War had become an established public figure, was still there at the age of 89, diligent and outspoken as ever, challenging from the Opposition Front Bench the Government's proposals for dealing with the economic situation. On that occasion he made his challenge with the mixture of forcefulness and moderation which was one of the many reasons for the respect in which he was universally held. For although he was by no means an uncontroversial figure, as indeed we on the Government Benches all had cause to know, the noble Lord's approach was always manifestly based, whenever he spoke, on certain fundamental moral principles in politics which I think would appeal to all your

Lordships' House: the need for all members of a society to be fair to one another the need for integrity in Government; the need for a people to be worthy if it is also to be great.[7]

The Labour peer Baroness Edith Summerskill added her own tribute:

In those days when he helped women to struggle for the franchise there were very few men who were prepared to face the ridicule, the ostracism and even the imprisonment which views of that kind often called for. But Pethick was a great man in the real sense, a man of stature. He was oblivious to ridicule. He simply regarded his principles as the light in his life. Few people know that for the last forty years after the struggle he has given of his great intellect, his money, his time and his energy to women's organisations which have been seeking to open other doors where women might express themselves fully. Pethick-Lawrence was a great gentleman of his generation, and the women of this country have lost a wonderful friend.[8]

Fourways was sold after Emmeline's death, although Fred kept the residential flat in Lincoln's Inn. But the local community in the Surrey Hills did not easily forget the Pethick-Lawrences, and it continued to honour them although not in perpetuity. In 1955, a year after Emmeline's death, the Labour Hall of which Fred had been the first president – at 85 South Street in Dorking – was re-named as Pethick-Lawrence House in Fred's honour. On 5 November 1955 the former prime minister Clement Attlee and his wife came down to perform the opening ceremony, at which Clement Attlee said that it was given to few men to play a major part in two great movements of liberation, as Fred had done.

A plaque erected on the headquarters of Dorking Labour Party in 1962 (itself named Pethick-Lawrence House) claimed that the work of Fred and Emmeline for the emancipation of women and for world peace 'would be remembered for countless generations.'[9] In the summer of 2022, however, the author made a pilgrimage to Dorking to look for for the Dorking and District Labour Halls. The building was still standing but the plaque was gone and it was no longer a Labour Halls but instead various offices, with no indication of what it had been. Dorking's excellent small Museum likewise has practically nothing on Fred and Emmeline. 'Countless generations' are clearly no longer being encouraged to remember the Pethick Lawrences in Dorking.[9]

A more poignant celebration followed on 7 July 1962, ten months after Fred's death, when the Suffragette Fellowship and a newly-formed Pethick-Lawrence Memorial Committee organised memorials in Dorking and Peaslake. Peaslake was decked out with suffragette colours, and a phalanx of very elderly surviving suffragettes – including Mary Leigh, Clara Codd (a suffragette and lecturer for the Theosophical Society 1878-1971), Joan Cruickshank, Lilian Lenton and Emmeline's sister Dorothy – made their way to its village hall to pay their respects. Tributes from Jawaharlal Nehru and Lord Mountbatten were read out, Joan Dugdale spoke about her life-long friendship with Fred and Emmeline, the Guildford Stoughton junior choir sang Jerusalem, and Clara Codd read the words of Fred's favourite hymn: 'When my mission is accomplished and my scroll complete/ thou will break this casket and gather me again unto thyself...'

Baroness Edith Summerskill then unveiled a portrait of Emmeline and Fred by the artist John Baker of Epsom. This was modelled on a photograph of an elderly Fred and Emmeline gathered around Fred's desk at Fourways, with the inscription 'In Memoriam. The Rt Hon Lord and Lady (Emmeline) Pethick-Lawrence of Peaslake'. At the base of the portrait there is a plaque with the poem Children of Freedom by the pioneering socialist and activist Edward Carpenter, who had been one of the people Emmeline most admired:

O Freedom Beautiful beyond compare,
Thy kingdom is established
Thou with thy feet on earth, thy brow among the stars, for ages us thy
                                        children
I, thy child, singing daylong, nightlong, sing of joy in thee.

Another plaque on the picture reads: 'Frederick William Pethick-Lawrence born 28 December 1871, died 10 September 1961/ Emmeline Pethick born 21 October 1867, died 11 March 1954/ In loving memory of Fred and Emmeline, Lord and Lady Pethick Lawrence of Peaslake, lovers of freedom and humanity whose combined work for the emancipation of women and for world peace will be remembered by countless generations'. The portrait had been sponsored by Viscount Alexander of Hillsborough, Frank Pakenham (the Earl of Longford), Dame Sybil Thorndike and Baroness Wootton of Abinger, who brought in many other contributors to pay for their various memorials. The portrait still has pride of place in Peaslake Village Hall, and it was proudly brought out into the sun to be photographed when I visited the hall in 2021.

On the evening of the day that the portrait was unveiled in Peaslake, Bernard Hunt of the Dorking Labour Party unveiled another portrait of Fred, also by John Baker, in Pethick-Lawrence House. In 1963 the Pethick-Lawrence Memorial Committee produced a pamphlet, *Memories of Fred and Emmeline Pethick-Lawrence*, and installed two memorial benches, one on Butter Hill in Dorking and the other on Holmwood Common, opposite the Sundial, where Emmeline had liked to sit years before. A local newspaper, the *Dorking Advertiser*, summed up Fred and Emmeline as a couple who 'never gave up, never relaxed, never despaired and are an inspiration for generations to come'.[10]

Immediately after Fred's death, a misunderstanding between his widow Helen and his two secretaries meant that quite a lot of his papers were inadvertently thrown away. So although the archive in the Wren Library at Trinity College, Cambridge, is extensive it is not complete.

In 2018 an image of Fred was one of only four male 'friends of the suffrage' to decorate the plinth below Gillian Waring's statue of Millicent Fawcett in Parliament Square: the first ever statue in the Square to depict a woman. This acknowledged the key role he had played in the struggle. This statue had been much fought for by the women's movement, and has become almost a place of pilgrimage.

Emmeline inspired devotion in many, including young men, with whom she could be quite flirtatious. She more or less adopted Annie Kenney and Christabel Pankhurst when they were young women, putting them up in her flat, and taking them on holiday on the continent. This was another cause for pain when the split with the Pankhursts came, and she and Fredf never saw Christabel again. Emmeline's life had great emotional highs but also a good deal of sadness.

Postscript

How do we ultimately assess Emmeline Pethick-Lawrence? By any measure she was a remarkable woman, who managed to extricate herself from the comfortable but constrained position of a middle-class Victorian daughter to develop a demanding career in social work, and then to organise and run the WSPU, one of the most successful – and challenging – organisations of its day, and become a powerful voice for peace. She had immense strengths, including courage, conviction, passion, leadership, creativity, financial acumen, organisational skills, and oratory.

Her friend Constance Lytton shared prison with Emmeline: and once wrote that 'I thought I had never seen a more attractive human being…',[1] and extolling her authority and leadership:

> I noticed with keener insight how remarkably the atmosphere of leadership clung around Mrs Pethick Lawrence. Her clothes and the disciplined routine were exactly the same in her case as in ours, she conformed to all the rules and seemed to adapt herself to the life as it had been of her choice and not imposed upon her. Yet the authority and, above all, the wisdom in her personality seemed to shine out more prominently even than they did in free life when she was controlling the many departments of the office at Clement's Inn for which she was responsible or of the public movement from a platform. Everyone came to her for advice, even the prison officers seemed instinctively to refer matters to her.[2]

But while Emmeline was completely whole-hearted and determined in her fight for votes for women – and for peace – she showed considerable failures of judgment in some of her other enthusiasms. The jury may be out on her relationship with Mark Guy Pearse but her relationships with John Hargrave, and the Kibbo Kift movement, Marie Stopes and the eugenics movement show indisputably bad judgement, albeit by benefit of hindsight. Similarly some of her more exaggerated mystical episodes (e.g. with spiritualism) come across as

Here were the headquarters of
THE WOMEN'S SOCIAL AND
POLITICAL UNION KNOWN
AS "THE SUFFRAGETTES"
LED BY EMMELINE AND
CHRISTABEL PANKHURST
Here also lived
EMMELINE PETHICK-LAWRENCE
WHO, WITH HER HUSBAND
PLAYED AN INVALUABLE PART IN
BUILDING UP THE ORGANISATION
AND EDITED "VOTES FOR WOMEN"

This plaque on a wall at the LSE commemorates the role of four key campaigners for the women's vote [Neville Grant]

completely 'over the top'. It should, however, be recognised that following the trauma of the First World War, many people sought meaning and purpose in spirituality by one route or another.

On a personal level Emmeline was in her youth both stylish and dashing. On their Golden Wedding in 1951 Fred recalled how he had married Emmeline because she smoked, could get off a moving bus, and didn't wear gloves whenever she went out for a walk, all of which marked her as a liberated woman.[3] She also sustained long and loving relationships – most notably of course with her husband Fred. Their marriage had its idiosyncrasies, but they were extremely devoted, and they were above all generous both to each other and others around them – generous with their time, money, houses and contacts.

Emmeline also sustained life-long and extremely affectionate relationships with other women, such as Mary Neal, who came down to live in Peaslake for the last few years of her life, with Sylvia Pankhurst (who was too upset to speak at her cremation), and with many others, such as Constance Lytton. And while she and Fred didn't have children of their own, Emmeline was extremely loving towards children.

The LSE re-named three of its Clement's Inn campus buildings after feminist campaigners: the other two are Pankhurst House, and Fawcett House

The Sundial, near the Mascot, was built particularly with children in mind and Emmeline considered all the children as part of her 'family'.

But possibly the most generous part of Emmeline's psyche was her capacity to forgive the Pankhursts for the egregious way they behaved when she and Fred were expelled from the WSPU. I don't think Fred and Emmeline ever forgot the slight, but they remained so determined not to damage the movement that they never spoke publicly against the Pankhursts, and Emmeline even corresponded with Christabel when she became a dame in the 1930s.

It is also true that after Emmeline's huge efforts first on behalf of votes for women, and then on behalf of peace, her participation in the

Feminism remains alive and well at the LSE, which now houses the Women's Library and archive

women's movement did dwindle as she grew older although her intervention with the Black and Tans in Ireland in the early 1920s was little short of heroic. From the mid-1920s onwards she was decreasingly active, even before a broken hip in 1950 immobilised her. Brian Harrison has described Emmeline as a 'lazy woman'. This description would not have been fair while she was running the WSPU, but in later life she certainly spent more and more time in bed, being waited on hand and foot by a phalanx of devoted attendants. It is easy to make fun of her as a follower of dead-end cults and religious sects, and to some, her exaggerated mysticism is reminiscent of Madame Arcati, the eccentric medium and clairvoyant in Noel Coward's 1941 play *Blithe Spirit*. But this does nothing to diminish her enormous achievements, and no one should fail to appreciate that she was a rounded human

Portrait of Fred and Emmeline at Fourways, painted from a photograph by John Baker. The painting hangs in Peaslake Village Hall

being, with faults and frailties as well as massive strengths. She had always been very sympathetic to other people's frailties, and she deserves the same sympathy as she got older.

Emmeline may have died nearly seventy years ago but she is not just remembered in the Surrey Hills. In honour of the anniversary of the Representation of the People Act, on November 23 2018 the LSE hosted a ceremony to inaugurate three residential students blocks: they are named them after three feminist campaigners, Emmeline Pankhurst, Millicent Garrett Fawcett and Emmeline Pethick-Lawrence. Pethick Lawrence House is the one nearest the Strand, on the site of Clement's Inn, and it is pleasing to know that today's young women now occupy the rooms from which Emmeline ran the WSPU so successfully more than a hundred years ago.

Notes

1. Early Years

1 Emmeline's autobiography (1938) *My Part in a Changing World*, (Victor Gollancz Ltd. 1938) p.50
2 *ibid* p.42
3 The Salvation Army, an evangelical Christian movement devoted both to the saving of souls and the relief of poverty, was founded in the East End of London in 1865 by William and Catherine Booth. Virulently anti-alcohol and tobacco, it aroused considerable animosity in the general public, and the police themselves were often hostile, In WW1, "the Sally Ann" was regarded as a true friend by front-line soldiers, and it is today much respected as an organisation that "puts faith into action" to help people in trouble,
4 *My Part In A Changing World*, p.65
5 *ibid* p.67
6 *ibid* p.70
7 *ibid* p.78
8 *ibid* p.72
9 *ibid* p.75
10 Mary Neal and Emmeline Pethick by Linda Martz, *Women's History Review*, 23:4 pp 620-641, p621
11 *ibid* p.621
12 *ibid* p.622
13 *Changing World*, p.84
14 *ibid* p.85
15 *ibid* p.86
16 v p.88
17 See Derek R. Williams, *Cornubia's Son: A Life Of Mark Guy Pearse* (Francis Boutle Publishers, 2008)
18 Mary Neal and Emmeline Pethick by Linda Martz, *Women's History Review*, 23:4 pp. 620-641, p.633
19 ibid p.630

2. Fred

1 *My Part in a Changing World*, p.123
2 Frederick Pethick-Lawrence's autobiography, *Fate Has Been Kind* (Hutchinson & Co, 1940)
3 *Fate Has Been Kind* p.15
4 *ibid* p.25
5 *ibid* pp. 28-29
6 *ibid* p.31
7 See lecture by Peter Blacker on The Cloisters at Letchworth and on Annie's subsequent career developing the Cloisters as an open-air school in psychology, which opened in 1907. (peter-blacker@virginmedia.com for further information)
8 *Fate Has Been Kind* p.44
9 *ibid* p.47
10 *ibid* p.51
11 *ibid* p.52
12 *ibid* p.53
13 Letter from Emmeline to Fred in 1900. Pethick-Lawrence Archive at the Wren Library, Trinity College, Cambridge) ref. 7/48
14 Hobhouse also became honorary secretary of the South African Women's and Children's Distress Fund, which she set up to improve conditions in which Boer civilians were held in the concentration camps.
15 *Fate has been Kind*, p.56
16 *ibid* p.58
17 *Changing World* p.124
18 Fate Has Been Kind p.60

19 *Changing World* p.94

20 *ibid* p.57

21 John Simkin (john@spartacus-educational.com) c September 1997 (updated January 2020. Accessed 23 October 2021)

22 Letter from Fred to Emmeline 22 January 1904; written from Trinity College, Cambridge (Wren Library Pethick-Lawrence Archive)

23 Letters from Fred to Emmeline April 1946. Archive at the Wren Library.

24 John Lawrence Hammond (1872-1949) was a journalist and writer on social history and politics. A number of his best-known books were written with his wife Barbara

25 Brian Harrison, *Prudent Revolutionaries* (Oxford: Clarendon Press 1985) p.243

26 Kathryn Atherton, *Suffragette Planners and Plotters: the Pankhurst, Pethick-Lawrence* Story (Pen and Sword, 2019)

3. 'An extraordinary outbreak at home…of disorder on the part of women'

1 A vivid description of Emmeline's trip to Egypt is contained in a blog put together by Adam Green of Trinity College Library. Cambridge
https://trinitycollegelibrarycambridge.wordpress.com/2021/09/06/three-women-in-a-boat/

2 I am grateful to the British Library's 2021 exhibition Unfinished Business: The Fight for Women's Rights for this information.

3 *My Part in a Changing World*, p.142

4 *ibid* p.148

5 cited in Shirley Harrison, *Sylvia Pankhurst: A Crusading Life 1882-1960* (London Arum Press 2003).p.66.)

6 Martin Pugh, *The Pankhursts* (Allen Lane, 2001), p149

7 *My Part in a Changing World*, p148

8 *ibid* p.149

9 *ibid* p.152

10 *ibid* p.152

11 *Women's Fight for the Vote* by Frederick Pethick-Lawrence (London: Woman's Press 1910; Published by Franklin Classics 2018) pp. 21-22

12 I am very grateful to Suzanne Keyte, archivist at the Royal Albert Hall, for this information.

13 *Changing World* p.168

14 Lucinda Hawksley, *March, Women, March: Voices of the Women's Movement* (Andre Deutsch, 2013)

15 *Changing World* p.169

16 *ibid* p.170

17 For a study of Millicent Fawcett's relationship with the WSPU, see Jane Grant's *In the Steps of Exceptional Women* (Francis Boutle Publishers 2016) Chapter 2 pp. 30-48

18 *Changing World* p.172

19 See *Christabel Pankhurst* by June Purvis (Routledge, 2018), p.105

20 See Sylvia Pankhurst's *The Suffragette Movement: An Intimate Account of Persons and Ideals - With an Introduction by Dr Richard Pankhurst* (Wharton Press 2020) p.252 Originally published in 1931.

21 *Changing World* p.177

22 *ibid* p.179

23 *ibid* p.179

24 *Hawksley*, op cit. pp.144-145

25 *Changing World* p.182

26 *ibid* p.184

27 *ibid* p.184

28 Quoted in *The Purple White and Green* by Diane Atkinson (Museum of London, 1992), p.15

29 *ibid* p15

30 *Changing* World p.188

31 *ibid* p.197

32 *ibid* p.199

33 Herbert Gladstone (1854 -1930) was the son of the former prime minister William Ewart Gladstone. After stepping down as Home Secretary in 1910 he was Governor-General of the Union of South Africa in 1910-1914.

34 *Changing World* p.200

35 *ibid* p.205

*

36 *ibid* p.205
37 *ibid* p.206
38 *ibid* p.207
39 Leaflet held in the archives of the Museum of London SO62/440/11
40 *Changing World*, p210
41 *ibid* p.214
42 *ibid* p.215
43 *ibid* p.215
44 *ibid* p.217
45 *ibid* pp.218-219
46 Emmeline Pethick-Lawrence's letters in the Wren Library, Trinity College Cambridge ref. 7/167
47 Constance Lytton: *Prisons and Prisoners: The Stirring Testimony of a Suffragette* (Virago, 1988) p.133
48 *ibid* p.152
49 Augustine Birrell (1850-1933) was a Liberal politician who had a keen interest in education and acted as Chief Secretary for Ireland in 1907-1916. While supportive of Mrs Fawcett's suffragists, he deplored the violence of the WSPU, and a damaged kneecap he sustained in 1910 was supposed to have been caused by aggressive suffragettes. He joked that he might as a result become a 'weak-knee-ed' politician
50 Wallace Dunlop (1864-1942) was a Scottish artist, author and suffragette. After being arrested for her action in St Stephens Hall she was one of the first, and most well-known, suffragettes to go on hunger strike in July 1909. She contributed her artistic skills to designing banners for the WSPU.
51 *Changing World* p.231
52 *ibid* p.233
53 *ibid* p.233
54 *ibid* p.236.
55 *ibid* p.237
56 *ibid* p.239
57   *ibid* p.240
58 *ibid* p.241
59 *ibid* p242
60 *ibid* p.244
61 *ibid* p.242
62 *ibid* p.246
63 Anne Cobden-Sanderson (1853-1926) was the daughter of the radical Richard Cobden. She added the name of her husband Thomas James Sanderson, a celebrated member of the Arts and Crafts movement, to hers on marriage. A suffragette and socialist, she was imprisoned and went on to help found the Women's Freedom League.
64 Princess Sophia Duleep Singh (1876-1948), a suffragette and a radical campaigner for women's rights, was the daughter of the deposed Maharaja Duleep Singh and a goddaughter of Queen Victoria.
65 quoted in *Hawksley* op cit p.166
66 *ibid* p.166
67 *Changing World* p.251
68 *ibid* p.252
69   *ibid* p.253
70   *ibid* p.254
 1   *ibid* p.260.
72 Sir Charles Hobhouse (1862-1941) was a British Liberal politician and a member of Asquith's Liberal cabinet in 1911-1915. He lost his Parliamentary seat in 1918.
73 *Changing World* p.264
74 *ibid* p.266
75 *ibid* p.270
76 As a nice footnote to this episode, the two daughters of the trial judge, Lord Justice Coleridge, subsequently applied for membership of the WSPU and subscribed to the campaign fund.
77 *The Daily News*, quoted in *Changing World* p.272
78 Letter in Wren Library. Trinity College Cambridge ref. 7/168
79 *Changing World* p.275

4. Things Fall Apart

 1 *My Part in a Changing World*, p.277 (The page numbers in Emmeline's book included a couple of misprints between pages 276 and 279.)
 2 *ibid* p.277

3	See chapters 13 and 14 of *Christabel Pankhurst: A Biography* by June Purvis (Routledge, 2018)
4	*Changing World* p.276
5	*ibid*.276
6	*Unshackled* by Christabel Pankhurst (Cresset Women's Voices, 1989), p.226 The book was originally published by Hutchinson in 1959.
7	*ibid* pp.225-229.
8	*Suffragette Planners and Plotters* by Kathy Atherton, p.132
9	*Changing World*, p.281
10	*ibid* p.282
11	Letter from Mrs Pankhurst to Emmeline Pethick-Lawrence, Wren Library, Trinity College Cambridge ref. 9/31)
12	Sylvia Pankhurst, *The Suffragette Movement* (Longmans Green & Co, 1931) p.222
13	*Changing World*, pp.284
14	*ibid* p.285
15	The plinth gives a list and images of 55 women including Emmeline Pankhurst, and her daughters Christabel and Sylvia – and Emmeline Pethick-Lawrence. The men listed are Fred, George Lansbury, Laurence Housman, and Claude Hinscliff.
16	*Changing World* p.285
17	Sara Jackson and Rosemary Taylor, *East London Suffragettes* (London: The History Press 2014) p.35
18	*The Suffragette Movement* p.174
19	*ibid* p.85
20	*ibid* p.85
21	From Emmeline's letter in the Wren Library ref 7VJH/1/4/07)
22	Quoted in Kathryn Atherton's *Suffragette Planners and Plotters* p.134
23	*Changing World* p.287
24	*ibid* p.288
25	*ibid* p.290
26	*ibid* p.292
27	*ibid* p.296
28	*ibid* p.297
29	Emily Wilding Davison was a teacher and governess who had been born in 1872 at Roxburgh House on Vanbrugh Park Road West in the south London suburb of Blackheath: by coincidence, just 500 yards from this author's current home.
30	*Changing World* pp.301-2

5. Peace Campaigner: 'Pow-Wows with the Fraus'

1	*Changing World* p.305
2	Sylvia Pankhurst's *The Suffragette Movement* (Longman Green and Co, 1931) p. 691
3	*Changing World*, p.306
4	Quoted in Adam Hochschild *To End All Wars* (Macmillan 2012) p. 140
5	*ibid*. p.313
6	*ibid* p.313
7	Report of the Hague Congress-
8	WILPF Constitution final, for presentation to Congress 8 March 2015 *WILPF: 100 Years, A Brief Look at a Long History* (WILPF, 2015)
9	*Changing World* p. 315
10	See *The Peacemakers: Six Months that Changed the World* by Margaret Macmillan (John Murray, 2001) p.21 passim
11	*Changing World*, p.316
12	*ibid*. p. 316 - 317
13	*Manchester Guardian*, 26 October 1918, under the headline 'The Latest Women's Victory'
14	The first woman to take an active role in the House of Commons was Nancy Astor, who became the member for Plymouth Sutton in 1919, after her husband Viscount Astor was elevated to the peerage.
5	*Changing World* p. 317
16	*ibid* p.322
17	*ibid* p.323
18	After Stoker's death in September 1919 a by-election in Rusholme was won by another Conservative, John Henry Thorpe – the father of the future Liberal leader Jeremy Thorpe.
19	*Changing World* p.323

20 *To End All Wars* p.355
21 Monica Siegal's *Peace on Our terms: The Global Battle for Women's Rights after the First World War* (Columba 2021)
22 *Changing World* p.326
23 *ibid* p.327
24 *Report of the International Congress of Women* p.17
25 See *A World Made New: Eleonor Roosevelt and the Universal Declaration of Human Rights* by Mary Ann Glendon (Random House, 2002)
26 *Report* op cit. p.56
27 *Report* p.61
28 *Report* pp.63-64
29 *Report* p.231
30 Letter from the archive of the Library of Manchester City Council Misc-78-99-101-0009. Thanks to Sarah Hobbes, the archivist, and Suzanna Caldicott the owner
31 Letter from the archive of the Library of Manchester City Council Misc-78-99-101-0009
32 *Report* p.154
33 *Report* p.156
34 *Changing World* p. 327
35 Margaret Macmillan, *Peacemakers: Six Months that Changed the* World (John Murray, 2001) p.500
36 Helen Kay is WILPF's long-standing and distinguished historian, and author of a forthcoming biography of the barrister Chrystal Macmillan, who had been a star of the two conferences.
37 David Diop has written a harrowing account of the horrors these troops experienced in his novel *At Night All Blood Is Black* (Pushkin Press, 2018)
38 *Report of Zurich Congress* p.224
39 *Changing World* pp.328 et seq.

6. Between the wars

1 *My Part in a Changing World*, p.336
2 *ibid* p.332
3 *ibid* p.333
4 *ibid* p.332. That organizations like the Six Point Group and the Open Door Council continued with these campaigns says a great deal about the failure of the Sex Disqualification (Removal) Act (SDRA) of 1919 to be properly implemented. Until 1945, women teachers had to resign when they got married; the Church of England had to wait until 2015 to get its first female bishop. Cambridge University did not award women degrees until 1948. In the 21st Century, the Fawcett Society still campaigns for equal rights for men and women.
5 Fred was nothing if not persistent – and successful: he stood for Parliament eight times: Aberdeen South as an independent in 1917 and then seven campaigns as a Labour candidate: Islington in 1922; Leicester West in 1923, 1924, 1929 and 1931, and in Edinburgh East 1935 and 1945. He was successful in 1923, 1924, 1929 and in 1935 and 1945, before being elevated to the Lords.
6 *Changing World* p.339
7 *ibid* p.340
8 Reports on the atrocities described appeared in the *Daily News* 27 April 1921 and 4 June 1921.
9 *ibid* p.342
10 *Changing World*, p.346
11 *ibid* p.349
12 *ibid* p.349-350
13 *ibid* p.351-2

7. Dreamer

1 *My Part In A Changing World*, pp. 350-352
2 *ibid*, p.43
3 *ibid* p.95
4 *ibid* p.88
5 *ibid* p.88
6 *ibid* p.94
7 *ibid* p.89

8   *ibid* p.100 Pages 100 – 111 indicate that this man who hated conflict, and preached love and reconciliation, was very influential even after the relationship faded .

9   *ibid* p.101

10 *ibid* p.102

11 *ibid* p.103

12 *ibid* p.104

13 *ibid* p.105

14 *ibid* p.108

15 *ibid* p.11

16 *ibid* p.109

17 Preface to *Changing World*, p.4

18 *op cit* p.285

19 *ibid* p.197

20 From a paper by Wendi Momen, *The Two Wings of Humanity: Abdu'l-Baha's Articulation of the Equality of Women and Men During His Western Travels*, given at the Hebrew University of Jerusalem in 2011, and before that at the Irfan Colloquium Session 97, Centre for Baha'i Studies, Acuto, Italy, on 3-4 July 2010 (abstract at http://irfancolloquia.org/97/momen_wings)

21 Alluded to in Promulgation of Universal Peace 375, quoted in Wendi Momen's paper

22 Promulgation of Universal Peace 172, quoted in Wendi Momen's paper

23 *Changing World*, p.326

24 Conference Report, p.230

25 *Suffragette Planners and Plotters*, p.126

26 *Suffragette Planners and Plotters*, p.126

27 *Suffragettes, Suffragists and Antis*, p.184

28 Mary Joannou, personal communication, 22 and 27 January 2022

29 I am indebted to Dr Annabelle Pollen's article 'A Society of Ugly People is an Immoral Society: Bodily Beauty in the Kindred of the Kibbo Kift' in Vestoj: Platform for Critical Thinking (2016), for much information about the Kibbo Kift. Dr Pollen is also the author of *The Kindred of the Kibbo Kift: Intellectual Barbarians* (Donlan Books, 2018) and she has written about exhibitions on 'The Kibbo Kift Kindred' at the Whitechapel Art Gallery in 1929 and 2015-2016.

30 Annabelle Pollen, *History Today* Vol 66 Issue 3, March 2016

31 *Suffragette Planners and Plotters*, p.126

32 I am grateful to Kathryn Atherton for this information.

33 Letter from Emmeline to Fred, 9 November 1904

34 Letter from Emmeline to Fred, 18 March 1946

35 Letter from Fred to Emmeline, 7 April 1946

36 Reprinted in Fate has Been Kind, p.9

8. In the Surrey Hills

1   Brian Harrison, *Prudent Revolutionaries: Emmeline and Fred Pethick-Lawrence* (Clarendon Press, 1987) p.253

2   *Changing World* p.324

3   Useful insights into the Pethick Lawrences' country houses were obtained by a day spent in the Surrey Hills with Kathy Atherton in May 2021, and from Kathy's two books: *Suffragettes, Suffragists And Antis: The Fight For The Vote In The Surrey Hills* (The Cockerel Press, 2017) and *Suffragette Planners And Plotters* (Pen and Sword, 2019) I am very grateful to Kathy for sharing her information with me.

4   *Suffragette Planners and Plotters*, p.36

5   *ibid* p.65

6   *Suffragettes, Suffragists And Antis* p.132

7   *ibid* p.136

8   *Suffragettes, Suffragists and Antis*, p,172

9   *Suffragette planners and plotters*, p.126

10 Suffragette interviews conducted by Brian Harrision (8SUF/B/097) The Women's Library.

11 I am grateful to Beverley Cook of the Museum of London for this information.

12 Letter in the Wren Library (2/39)

13 Margaret Haig Thomas, Lady Rhondda (1883-1958) was a stalwart of the women's movement between the wars. Amongst many other activities she founded the Six Point Group and the Open Door Council, and she edited the feminist periodical *Time and Tide*. See Chapter 6. Some of the issues raised are still being pursued by other women's organisations such as the Fawcett Society.

14 *Prudent Revolutionaries*, p.257

9. Towards India

1   Brian Harrison's *Prudent Revolutionaries* (Oxford: Clarendon Press 1985) p.263-264
2   During World War Two, in 1942, as a member a small splinter group from the Labour Party that opposed war, Frederick Pethick-Lawrence briefly acted as Leader of the Opposition. (Attlee and other senior Labour politicians became members of the coalition government.)
3   From the *Times*' Obituary of Fred quoted in Vera Brittain, Pethick-Lawrence: a Portrait (George Allen and Unwin, 1963) p142
4   Quoted in Vera Brittain's *Pethick-Lawrence A Portrait* (George Allen Unwin, Ltd 1963) p.135
5   *op cit* p.136
6   *op cit* pp.135-136
7   Swarajists were members of the Indian National Congress, or Congress Party. In 1923 they formed a separate party within the Congress Party. The Swarajists were led by M. Nehru and C. Das.
8   A full account of their visit can be found in Chapter 10 of Brittain's book, pp.135 – 142.
9   *Brittain*, p138
10 *op cit* p146
11 *op cit* p161
12 For a detailed account of Pethick-Lawrence's role, and the aftermath, see R. J. Moore's 'Mountbatten, India and the Commonwealth' in the *Journal of Commonwealth Studies* 1981 19:1 pp 5-43
13 Quoted in *Brittain*, p.187. Dr Gooch was a distinguished British journalist, historian and Liberal Party politician.
14 A staunch supporter of a united India, he was President of the INC from 1940-1945, and Minister of Education after independence until his death in 1957.
15 5/69e – Letter from Wren Library, Cambridge, the Pethick-Lawrence archive.
16 *Hansard*, 17 October 1961

10. The Final Curtain

1   From the chapter on Emmeline and Fred Pethick-Lawrence in Brian Harrison's *Prudent Revolutionaries*, (Oxford: Clarendon Press 1987) p.254
2   Their friendship runs like a seam through Sylvia's latest, and largest, biography: *Sylvia Pankhurst: Natural Born Rebel* by Rachel Holmes (Bloomsbury Publishing, 2020).
3   In the WREN Library archives, and quoted in Sylvia Pankhurst's, *Natural Born Rebel* March 1954 p.742.
4   *Suffragette Planners and Plotters* p.139
5   *Pethick-Lawrence: A Portrait*, p.211
6   *ibid* p.212
7   *Hansard*, 17 October 1961
8   *ibid*
9   Countless generations? A visit to Dorking in August 2022 revealed 85 South Street is still standing but now as a location for various offices rather than a Labour Rooms (it was sold several years previously). There is no plaque or record at all of its previous life as a Labour building, its re-naming as Pethick-Lawrence House, or the visit by Prime Minister Clement Attlee.
10 *Suffragettes, Suffragists and Antis*, p.201

Postscript

1   *Prison and Prisoners*, p.81
2   *ibid* p.153
3   *News Chronicle* (2 October 1951)

Bibliography

Atherton, Kathryn: *Suffragette Planners And Plotters: The Pankhurst, Pethick-Lawrence Story*. Pen & Sword, 2019

Atherton, Kathryn: *Suffragettes, Suffragists And Antis: The Fight For The Vote In The Surrey Hills*. The Cockerel Press, 2017

Brittain, Vera: *Pethick-Lawrence: A Portrait*. George Allen & Unwin, 1963

Crawford, Elizabeth: *The Women's Suffrage Movement: A Reference Guide 1866-1928*. Routledge, 1999

Glendon, Mary Ann: *A World Made New: Eleonor Roosevelt and the Universal Declaration of Human Rights*. Random House, 2001

Harrison, Brian: 'The Politics Of A Marriage' in *Prudent Revolutionaries – Portraits Of British Feminists Between The Wars*. Clarendon Press, 1987

Harrison, Shirley, *Sylvia Pankhurst: A Crusading Life 1882-1960*, London, Aurum Press, 2003

Hawksley, Lucinda: *March, Women, March: Voices Of The Women's Movement From The First Feminist To The Suffragettes*. Andre Deutsch, 2013

Hochschild, Adam: *To End All Wars: A Story Of Protest And Patriotism In The First World War*. Pan Books, 2012

Holmes, Rachel: *Sylvia Pankhurst: Natural Born Rebel*, Bloomsbury Publishing, 2020

Houses of Parliament: *Parliament and Votes for Women*, Parliamentary Archives, Undated

Jackson, Sarah, and Taylor, Rosemary: *East London Suffragettes*. The History Press, 2014

Lytton, Constance: *Prisons and Prisoners: The Stirring Testimony of a Suffragette*. Virago, 1988 (first published in 1914)

Macmillan Chrystal, et al. (Eds) *Women Vote Peace: Zurich Congress 1919:* Zurich 2019, Women's International League of Peace and Freedom

Margaret Macmillan, *Peacemakers: Six months that changed the World*, John Murray, 2001

Martz, Leah: *Mary Neal and Emmeline Pethick – From Mission to Activism*. Women's History Review, 2014, Vol 23 No 4 pp620-641

Pankhurst, Christabel: *Unshackled: The Story Of How We Won The Vote*. Hutchinson, 1987 (first published 1959)

Pankhurst, Sylvia: *The Suffragette Movement*. Longmans Green and Co, 1931

Pethick-Lawrence, *Emmeline: My Part in a Changing World*. Victor Gollancz, 1938

Pethick-Lawrence, Frederick: *Fate Has Been Kind*. Hutchinson & Co, 1942

Pethick-Lawrence, Frederick: *Women's Fight for the Vote*. The Woman's Press, 1910 (reprinted by Franklin Classics)

Pugh, Martin, *The Pankhursts*, Allen Lane, 2001

Purvis, June: *Christabel Pankhurst: A Biography*. Routledge, 2018

Takayanagi, Mari (Editor): *Voice And Vote: Celebrating 100 Years Of Votes For Women*. Regal Press Ltd, 2018

Williams, Derek R: *Cornubia's Son: A Life Of Mark Guy Pearse*. Francis Boutle Publishers, 2008

Index